THE NEW ARCADIA

ALSO BY JOHN KINSELLA

POEMS

Peripheral Light
The Hierarchy of Sheep
Zone
Visitants
The Benefaction
The Hunt
Poems 1980–1994
Graphology
Lightning Tree
The Undertow
The Radnoti Poems
The Silo: A Pastoral Symphony
Erratum / Frame(d)
Syzygy
Full Fathom Five
Eschatologies
Night Parrots

FICTION

Grappling Eros
Genre

DRAMA

Divinations: Four Plays

AUTOBIOGRAPHY

Auto

THE NEW ARCADIA

⟨⟨⟨⟨ POEMS ⟩⟩⟩⟩

John Kinsella

W. W. NORTON & COMPANY
New York • London

For information about permission to reproduce selections from this book, write to
Permissions, W. W. Norton & Company, Inc., 500 Fifth Avenue, New York, NY 10110

Manufacturing by Quebecor Fairfield
Book design by Brooke Koven

Library of Congress Cataloging-in-Publication Data

Kinsella, John, 1963–
The new Arcadia : poems / John Kinsella.— 1st ed.
p. cm.
ISBN 0-393-06053-5 (hardcover)
1. Western Australia—Poetry. 2. Landscape—Poetry. I. Title.
PR9619.3.K55N49 2005
821'.914—dc22

2005004427

W. W. Norton & Company, Inc., 500 Fifth Avenue, New York, N.Y. 10110
www.wwnorton.com

W. W. Norton & Company Ltd., Castle House, 75/76 Wells Street, London W1T 3QT

1 2 3 4 5 6 7 8 9 0

for Susan Stewart

DEDICATION

Flanking or hedging in,
the twenty-eights hurry
us through lines of back-roads,
linking sullen and bright
trees, liquid in changing
weather, monitoring
pace and direction,
shifting dispositions.

The author wishes to acknowledge
the traditional owners of the lands he writes.

Arcadia among all the provinces of Greece was ever had in singular reputation, partly for the sweetness of the air and other natural benefits, but principally for the moderate and well tempered minds of the people who (finding how true a contentation is gotten by following the course of nature, and how the shining title of glory, so much affected by other nations, doth indeed help little to the happiness of life) were the only people which, as by their justice and providence gave neither cause nor hope to their neighbours to annoy them, so were they not stirred with false praise to trouble others' quiet, thinking it a small reward for the wasting of their own lives in ravening that their posterity should long after say they had done so.

—from SIR PHILIP SIDNEY'S
The Countess of Pembroke's Arcadia

CONTENTS

ACT 1

ACT 2

ACT 3

ACT 4

THE LAST ACT (5)

Envoy

ACKNOWLEDGMENTS

Previously uncollected poems have appeared in:

Landfall, Southern Review, London Review of Books, The Artful Dodge, Agenda, Tears in the Fence, Rue Bella, The New England Review, Salt, Leviathan, Denver Quarterly, Thylazine, TriQuarterly, The Mid-American Review, Agni, Michigan Quarterly Review, Poetry Review, Southwest Review, The Boston Review, The Literary Review, The Idaho Review, Fulcrum, Notre Dame Review, Quarterly West, World Literature Today, Poetry London, Australian Book Review, Washington Square, The Age, Grand Street, The New Orleans Review, The Carolina Quarterly, Overland, The North, Agni, Prairie Schooner, Ars Interpres, Smartish Pace, The Iowa Review, The Best Australian Poems (2003), *Salmagundi, Conduit.*

Thanks to Kenyon College, Churchill College (Cambridge University), and ECU, for ongoing support, and special thanks to my partner, Tracy Kinsella.

A number of the 'bird' poems included in this work originally appeared in a one-off 'illuminated' manuscript illustrated by the author's brother and given to the author's partner as a birthday gift.

ACT 1

REFLECTORS: DRIVE 1

At The Lakes, the V takes you away
from the traffic, though accidents
happen up this way as well,
the surge upwards and decline,
from cryptic entanglements
of salmon gums—brief
but intense stands bristling
on high ground, to ghostly trunks
of spotted gum, where firebreaks
then paddocks striate between gravel
and sand. This is the drive to York,
repetition, imprint of incursion
and memory, unwinding daily.
Where you say: we are moving
away from the city, and only
the notion is boutique. At dusk,
leadlit clouds hum at a distance, at a place
not quite the horizon. The bush
can only appear uneasy, as fences
indicate eventual clearing—astonishing
when the salt has them reafforesting
cleared ground frantically,
out of time with manic erosion.
These are things you might think or say
but you drive on, because you
have to—sparks in pistons,

tapping inside the engine, exhaust
that works against air and cartels.
We forget this and make it an aside
as the light closes off and a rare
native cat dashes across the road
as if it were the early hours
of the morning. The grace of swerving
within the river of asphalt,
gathering luminescence of cat's eyes
and reflectors on the shoulders.
People measure lives here by miles
they've chewed up—some never
leave town, and they are the centre
of the compass. The point
from which all measurements
are taken. In the rush, it's a picture
of a flow, but repeated crossings
with a particular tree, a curve
in the road, a Ray White 'For Sale' sign
that tilts lower and lower
with each journey—it all comes up close.
Exposure means zoom. Macro, micro,
wide angle. Through windows, windscreen . . .
passing a car, overtaking a truck . . .
just taking it easy, dawn or dusk,
midday, deep in the night, high summer
when upholstery strips away,
cracking and blistering, roadhaze
intense enough to twist your sense
of real or imagined, in the slough
of a wet winter, even the comfort zone
of a perfect spring. It varies. As

stripped-back it unfocusses, a clarity
of undoing evolves. You age with it,
it ages you, you know it closely.
The crosses have multiplied: four
on that bend, one with a motorcycle helmet;
just outside York a memorial to an ex-
bikie who became a JP and the best-loved
citizen of the community. A moment
serves as a volta, a point of delay:
the cops pulling up for a wreath-laying
on the anniversary of his death.
Witness: the slow drive past,
their pulling in, their wreath
glowing quietly on the return journey.
The road is gender and cinema,
and the 13 Mile Brook an indicator
of contemplation, the 6 Mile Brook
one of intensity, a nearing of the end
of your journey, which are all bound
in one. And conceptually, the city
is the undercurrent, the driver
that propels the degradation
and renewal of the road, on and on.
Heading back, going home, it's the sight
of Mount Bakewell that acts chemically,
the fluctuation of serotonin levels,
flutter of eyelids as some joker
fails to dip highbeam and dazzles
you—the mountain hidden,
but you know it's there: compulsive,
creating weather, full of contradictions.
The hill of tears, sullen centre.

Centres of gravity, the car adheres
around tight slowdown bends,
through Cut Hill, past straggling
York gums, shedding their bark
and shining though it might be winter.
The seedling crops crisping, curling
on their gentle furrows, slight
upraisings running as parallelograms
across the paddocks, winding across
rock piles and the odd marri tree.
Earlier rains brought no follow-up
and the choking soil shrivels
and dries with frost. Fog is just
torture, like a snatch of air
when you're drowning. That moment
before the accident. Crops are ploughed
back in, from Wambyn Nature Reserve cut-
off, to the outer wheatbelt. Everything's
a risk. Reflectors confuse night-trawling
tractors, red markers slow in fields,
the left—red hypnotics,
the right—silver dazzle,
repetition and persistence.
And soon, in the gulley at home,
magpies and kookaburras compete,
galahs spread out over the desiccated drills,
it's dusk. Multiple species with delicate
variations. Hakea bush cuts shadow.
The charge: myths of robustness,
of making a go of it. They just die
when the spray drifts, when rains
have brought crops. On the mountainside

they collect data on residue. Static.
A black spot. Radio drops out,
you switch from FM to AM,
go mono. National news.
Fate of IT stocks, special news
for primary producers.
Synchronicity, it colludes
with the sheep truck, vulvas
of ewes hanging through the gridwork . . .
gender. Three kilometres until
the passing lane. The semi-trailer
a sick ship, a warped biographia
literaria. There's a lot of bad poetry
here: the truck's name is *Michael*,
Hellraiser—that's what you see
in the mirror as you pass, blue perspex
on the bonnet reversing itself naturally
in the mirror, like code. Encrypt:
pink glare of eucalypts at twilight,
as if all light comes from within
and slips down contours, depressions
in the country. Twenty-three ks
of kangaroo stretch from the V,
though the forest thinning
and few corpses. In childhood
you wouldn't have been driven
along this route without a roo bar
out front. It deserves no adjective.
But stray appearances are made,
and even in winter a grey roo corpse
will swell up and burst, carrionpoint
for foxes and crows. We read:

aerial baiting of foxes has begun
for the season. The season . . .
failed plantings, resentment.
What are we nostalgic for?
We? Family? *They* were relatively
'good to the natives' when they first arrived
mid-nineteenth century, a respected family.
Some are part of the Nyungar family
now, though it's denied. *Our* family
employed Nyungars as stookers,
rime riche in the windrows,
respecting their abilities,
and it being economic.
As they pertained.
They, we, pertained. To crop
the hay. *Who* writes in their head
as they drive, the car the head
of a dreaming snake, cutting out
the sluice of the Avon Valley, allowing
the built-up water to flow away.
To the sea. Survey maps. Photographs.
Stories that get taken and retold.
Theft is history, metaphor
assimilation. Sheep feeders
hover over paddocks. Never
roos here, or rarely. Farmers
are investing in emus, which run
fences and strike, as if at cars.
The sheep feeders, alien vessels.
Beyond reflectors, almost weekly
sightings. Witnesses. All about light
and darkness and markings on cleared

lands. They appear where there's
a clearing—sightings increase
incrementally. A burning off,
orange flames excoriate, scorching
fractious genealogies into tableau,
vista: mesmeric, you decelerate
and smell woodsmoke through a partially
opened window, though it's so far off
you might be imagining it. But not
that far—there are no horizons,
only light, darkness, the gaseous
states in between. A fireball
erupts and the woodtype is suspected:
a massive mallee root, a reservoir
of moisture, air pockets. Crack!
It's an emotional moment.
And then, it is empty, burning
only as afterimage. Figuratively,
it connects to nothing.
There's no language.
The wings joined together,
night a crow, its eye hollow.
Passengers, maybe four of them,
alike and different. Spiritually,
physically. Anglican, Catholic, Muslim,
and Buddhist. Get their age and gender,
the graphologist suggests, he or she
examining the signatures
in their passports. Look, this
is the country someone else stole
but we make good use of; we said
sorry, and marched intermittently.

Hardwood burns hot here,
winters are mild. In summer
a lack of shade will leave your skin
to cancer. They say: slip, slop, slap.
Fact. Factor. Factotum.
The moon is rarely this thin,
stars deflecting town light.
The house coming into sight,
the picture a genre of presence:
materials, light and dark, fire-resistant
and combustible. In the wet
it turns into a quagmire,
but it's okay to park here
in spring or autumn.

PYTHIC SMALL BIRDS ARE THE POINT WHERE WANDOO AND YORK GUM GIVE WAY TO JAM TREE, THE GRANITIC HILLS GENTLY CLIMBING

Trip-wire and tilt,
    flipping and paralleling
        when all was silent;
wasted in our frippery
    they changed the sun, our colours
        washed to soil and water, running
into each other, blending.
    We wanted and they short-circuited
        shadow as bright as dazzle,

flash-blindness placing dark
    absorbent spots on the luminous
        object. Lichen moves on jam tree,
a slight behind us. Onion grass
    laminates the breeze it captures,
        so much caught in our language.
Little corellas follow an adjacent
    tree-line—their lustre
        all sound. We sense confidence.
We do not feel uncomfortable
    in our bodies, though can't be sure
        they're centres of calm.
Conflict dissipates with denudation.
    We can't ask her as air
        that sears vocal chords is unfamiliar,
words taken by smaller birds:
    dusted yellow, black hoods,
        the finch-like beaks of wedge politics?
A redwood bends to compliment
    the granitic hills, once green-boned
        and gently climbing, retro
as York gum and wandoo,
when all was silent we were.

A FRONT APPROACHES

Clear. Flowering gums strobe red, quick
    with the breeze. The phthalo blue
        sky makes silhouettes

of mountain, trees.
The glow offensive, the light screws

subcutaneous, burns roots:
    the sharp black-faced cuckoo-shrike
        committed to that
        dead-limb pivot—
cantilevered, gyroscopic

legs working below body,
    to touch the edge of the front,
        driven up askew
        as darkly through
leaf-swatches it charts its ascent.

RAIN GAUGE

Millpoint throaty guzzler, wishful
choker as dust films throat, to measure up,
squalls with hooks and introversions, bale-hooks,
moebius comeback though sharp and sliced
from the same stretch, to hang up or catch skin
to ripen blood-eating earth, so sharp needles
of rain crosscut, score soil and tease seeds,
to calibrate the empty out and add up,
it says enough but penetration's not there
and lateral spread, its absorption
which is not a formula of depth, width, impact,
even with the resistance, the failure of soil
to wet, taken into consideration. What factor
has us check the gauge when the crops are in,

when growth is simply about moisture,
to engage the rainmaker, the seeder of air
when airseeders have percolated hectare
after hectare of earth, to balance the equation,
the anti-matter or parallel universe of planting
and growth, the balanced equation of faith
that adds up so each seed sprouting
spites and despites the rain gauge
as if miracles can blossom from the negative?
They can't, and even moisture from the sea
won't reconcile tropes and impositions,
and the miracle of rain we might not even see
will be seen in crops and wild grasses,
good foliage on even hardy resistant trees,
less salt in low damp spots—an adjustment
in contradictions, apparent laws
we apparently live by, bothering the gauge
after sleep's deliberations, blanks, and deletions.

CLEANING THE NEW RAINWATER TANK DURING THE ONSET OF AN ELECTRICAL STORM . . .

1. Scene

John's cleaning the new rainwater tank
Tracy and I have bought by way of thanks
to Mum for making this place possible;
it's concrete and an oily film floats

on top of the 'one rung's' worth of rain
that's fallen in early summer. There
are thunderheads about so it's likely
we'll get more and the red light
from behind the mountain
unsettles the black-purple fringe
stacked on the horizon. So John's
scrubbing it clean with a brush
and flushing it down through the brass
tap with the hose, even washing
down the shed roof at my request
to prevent Roundup spray residue
from the neighbour's lazy
and indifferent firebreak-making.
There's a peal of thunder and we rush
out as forks of lightning stretch
over the district, clawing
their way down to the paddocks,
reaching towards town in the distance.
It's sudden and dark and night
smashes into cloud too heavy
to stay afloat. We call to John
to get out and as he does it comes
down in buckets. A driving rain
that'll wash away the gravel track.
He stands there with lightning
prising apart silver and gold fillings,
lifting fingernails, turning spinal cords
to charcoal. Shep the Kelpie
is howling inside and Mum and Tracy
are saying 'Get in! Get in!'

There are yelps of horror and delight
from neighbouring properties
as trees and granite silhouettes
erupt, it's all that loud. John,
drenched to the skin, climbs up on to the tin roof
to watch the water flow into the tank:
'A summer's worth in minutes!'
he yells as the forks turn to sheet
and bathe the whole place in religious light.

2. Summary

The tank was laid
and hooked to the shed's
guttering, an electrical storm
lighting up the district,
he managed to prepare
it just in time:
they had water to see
out the summer.

3. Ellipsis

Criticised for not having cleaned the tank
before connecting the gutter, he'd gone out in a storm
to make sure the others weren't disappointed.
He pours a drink of rainwater and offers
it to taste . . .

4. Descriptive Pause

At *that* moment, lit up
grey concrete shows
that light doesn't work in all places
on all surfaces, overhanging
eucalypts burning oil in their cells
as lightning heats air, though appears
cold, cold as the corrugated iron roof
of the shed, slightly blue metal
of guttering, all these told
by static, by the night-sight
of recall; the pressed flat disc
of yellow sand upholding a whorled
concrete cylinder, odd chips
of discretion shed elsewhere,
hint of wire mesh,
incongruities of the mould,
some of it on the workshop floor,
not here under the electric storm,
windows glazed with reversals
of form: Calcinatio, Solutio,
Coagulatio, Sublimatio . . . Coniunctio,
as fused as prayer, an outline
of someone poised, stratagem
inlaid as ingot or stele or reservoir,
furnace fired against barbed wire,
stacks of red brick dampening
insect-eruptions, drawn to the yellow
verandah light, clicking on thin
curved glass, engorged droplet

of vacuum, light held up
by what's not transmutation
on this night of cleaning,
getting ready; bristling and stuck-up
in its echo, this echo hissing and crackling, yes, yes,
perceived its vertigo, this outline of tools,
brush in hand, shovel with split handle
and worn blade against the tank, a foothold
for coming down, but still poised,
hammer for a task unrelated
but there in the storm,
perceptible when things light up
brighter than the bulb on the verandah
can cast.

THE SWING

To make portions of the circle
the mountain draws you up, and granite
in slabs and lumps draws you back,
radiant in this sector, kick-off

point the tangent of compulsion
against which you swing, prayer mat
that shifts you out of the arc,
saying gravity   gravity   gravity

is far from up and down, there and back,
it tenses chords of sound strung from branches,
observer upwind or down laughing, goading
you on. Swing   swing   swing

to piece colour into the story,
make light loud and not of sight,
grow tired when you're most awake
and forget that love ever motivated

waking up, or attempting to sleep
enough hours of the night. A bird
strikes as you're on the rise,
a threat or response to fright;

the mountain blurs into the gulley
and clouds are firebreaks laid bare
by Roundup; breathing out, then breathing
out, there's no space for air,

and shadows are suns compressed in grass,
heat sucked dry and turned like negatives:
place heaves against the linchpin, centre-bar
the horizon around which we flatly rotate.

THE RURAL STAGE

These surging backdrops, proscenium,
indulge keyhole looping round Needling Hills,
forbidden now though language is made up out of it,
and moments that can't be undone: this not stepping
into profit and holdall, images and iconoclasts, a real-
    estate
agent at Nicene insisting spray was last used here

ten years ago, this fertilising body a sack
of residue, the car shacking down to bare bits
over corrugations where dryandra is thick
on roadsides, a gravel-pit reclaiming itself
and sandplain thinning crops across the dividing
media of road, a snapping futchel, differential
split, custos, this court-case
to determine flows beneath our wheels,
indeed our feet, oubliette households
where sparks fire qualms and gardyloo,
the poet Brockman who wrote of this purple
mountain not far from here, not far
from what appears eudemonism,
teleports for Mercedes-Benz,
but in fact obsession and a knowing
that has them lashing out, that will
see them thin on the ground
when there are no varieties
of wheat hardy enough
to sustain encomiums,
the rural.

NO MOMENT IS WASTED

Broad leaf-blade, cuttingly green,
attenuating dryness, scansion of grasses
papered, brittle, entangled by southerlies
and the motifs of heat: waves teasing out
cell walls, making clouds too thin

and fine to see; so here, sense
the racehorse goanna hesitating
outside its burrow, its skin
rough before shedding, leaching
sunlight, offloading shadows
that force one foot above rough earth
inlaid with quartz, cool and comfortable
perched on eclipse: this moment elsewhere,
as crimes of pleasure or addiction
might confer: here, this goanna
sunning by the roadside,
low frequency of traffic
not driving deep into bush . . .
but company fails to notice,
as if it just goes to show
the sun unbalances,
or shifts emphasis,
and not shadow.

THE SWORD OF AESCULAPIUS

The twist of the bird-like
seed—spiral affixer,
host-searcher, travel-bugged
itinerant, peripatetic freeloader,
mechanism taking its chance,
latency enraptured: to soil-burrow,
self-bury through efficiency,
to awaken after the chance taken:

and so to work my sock
and beyond a temporal point,
sword-tip, angering skin
and what lies within,
much of me running out
along cold steel barb,
irritant undermining
chit-chat and flowerings
farther afield.

TILT

Iron telegraph mazurka
lineless hipster, anachronistic
swinger that's got away, low as limbo
a lightning skewer, this Olympian
wormhole in paddocks of irony: metal shavings
from beneath the patent zimmer in the warm-enough
almost sun, a pataphysical operator, New Age guru
in the volatile oil of heated eucalypt
sharing a common root: termites glance
off its bolder façade, the rust of earth
making lines and lures, the wagtail
risking the road a stone's throw away,
new sheds rising, getting larger;
so tilt, tilted against the loquacity
of sitting water, mosquitoes flurrying
the green, the urge of the mid-range:
tweeters cutting into sub-woofers

alter with tilt, the vehicle
without wheels angle-grinding
its rest-place, from where
all windscreens slant against shade thrown
by slightly heavier clouds
congregating about the spindles
of prayer-meisters come together, angled congenitally
even when the TV's reception is shaky.

THEY SAY OF BATS . . .

They can make you fear all creatures:
scare tactics, the bat that will tangle
in your hair after sunset, need to be hacked
out with scissors, claws and bones
and membranes knotted down, veins
plugging into the skull, filling
follicles and biting thought-patterns
with alliteration; the short distance
between air and skin layer that touches
the hemisphere of skull, asymptotic,
is the black transparency of a batwing
stretched against dull luminance of a town
or light burning deep below the rim
of horizon, a faint memory or gesture,
sometimes filled with spite, the day
not quite going right; and the teeth
they'll call rabid where no rabies
has been reported, an agility without sight

that makes a corrupt diagnosis;
and fear mythologises like 'trinkets
dangling from an elderly woman's
once glamorous neck', these miniature
beasts always threatening to grow larger
than the sky will take, come down
out of cavities in trees and hillocks,
festeringly social in their own communities,
yet, we're warned, smothering ours,
quick to die in your hair,
get under your skin.

EXTREME CONDITIONS OCCASION THE FOX

Red nightclouds suspended over treetops
send a shiver up the spine, searching
for oncoming headlights—nothing.
And suddenly, through Rorschach-sheoaks
the moon, late in rising, trepans
into paddocks, incipient surfaces—soaks
and dams its drainage, macabre and ghoulish.
X-raying the brain, they photograph slices,
slices of the moon, the z and a, synecdoche
of waxing and waning: expressionist, anaemic,
shadow-libations in the granite agora, acidic
tracks resonant in deficient soil. Naples yellow,
powdered orange, bisque, and climbing rapidly:
mimesis. Massive haystack near the turn-off—
steady and municipal by daylight—listless,

heaving slowly into the spreading afterglow.
Instantly the fox, twist plot, stops
mid-sentence: roadside reflectors framing
it like scare quotes, drought feeding
self and projections, laid out in the valley.

DEAD WOOD AND SCORPIONS

Split, sliced, shattered—petrified tailings
spilling termites. Fallen jam tree
harbouring bull-eyed lizards
in the paddock, tail-less
implication of words
grubbing for transcriptions.

In the wicker basket,
the trendy or cheap woodbox,
fashion victim,
miniature scorpions slide
out from flakes, crusts
of bark; on the tiles

scuttling works: this bigotry,
tail oscillating as if electric,
a casing of nerves,
impulses. Or a fuse
lit but latent—
heart's spike—

or just another jag
of conscience. Two emerged—
last night? Like land-clearing machinery
lurking just over the rise
on Uncle Jack's old property—
or nothing like it.

Segmented body—rolls of wood,
splinters, symmetry.
An order of burning,
strewn in and through and under
flames. The sting,
hot on skin, in blood.

THE BUNGARRA GOANNA

The yellow spots
of the bungarra
connect Walwalinj
and Babylon; at a glance
there are eighty-nine
and they're golden.
Poised at the mouth
of its burrow, it takes
the last increment of sun,
its golden ratio
of conglomerate, red dirt,
and swirls of dead grass.
Days quickening

it varies its descent,
though we wait,
give or take scales
packed like a sunflower,
or the native plant
not counted on, packed
into the sun which is easiest
to look into at close of day
not long from now,
and not for long.

180 DEGREES OF SEPARATION

The sheep came here before entering the yard
for the killing: he would cut their throats

with a short, worn knife. I have written
about this in a variety of ways. I keep

rewriting the same poem. But there were
many occasions I *witnessed*—the word's

appropriate—and a book entirely composed
of poems about sheep killing would not

be enough. Maybe a line for each organ?
A page for each carcass? A section for the skins

laid out over the fence—oily and yellow inside.
The wool shorn back to the uncoloured outer skin

month after month. Years. Decades.
He kept the freezer full of sheep parts.

I'm sure he didn't enjoy what he did—it was work.
He noted the pigs enjoyed the innards

dumped from the barrow. The cold brought
steam, the heat a stink that permeated.

An outdoor task—below the shed overhang—
for all weathers. The frightened bleated like a storm.

What I've not considered is the shape
of the paddock where the sheep selected for killing

waited out their time. Only a few, the feed
was rarely under pressure. A triangular paddock,

its angles went from relatively open to suffocation.
The sheep, I recollect, rarely grazed in the narrow

point—the angle furthest away from the killing yard
and slaughter hook. They moved on trails looped

across the broad end of the field, the end nearest the dirt
with its red inside red: like oil-stains that go a long way

below the surface, sit on the water table. Float.
I wonder if the shape of the paddock was coincidence

or convenience: the mathematics of bottlenecks
and imperative, the sides always adding up: the half-life,

the lifting out of the herd: there was no random
gesture in the killing, and the prejudice

was lost as good people grew used to it.
Forgive them Lord, they know not what they do?

THE TELEPHONE PADDOCK

It's easy to say 'this one is for you'—
it's a convention, what all fathers-to-be would do

if insomniac and sweltering with summer
humidity at three in the morning. Gambier,

Ohio—you'll be born here, your home. But where
I'm from it's hesitating towards winter,

the rains playing out their most-years ritual
of holding off, the seasons getting later and less literal:

winter means autumn and spring winter,
but a shorter version thereof. They say you're

what's called a 'late child', a wonderful surprise.
I won't argue with that, and the risk of sunrise

being muted by storms makes me more
rather than less optimistic. I digress: the store

of what makes me is distracted by a picture
I can see clearly behind my eyes: though I'm unsure

of the boundaries between memory
and something I've configured through free

association: maybe it's to do with the society
I'm in? Being of both places, your identity

will be informed by such tensions. An email
from your great auntie reminds me of a family tale:

when she was pregnant with one of the cousins
she spoke on the not-long-connected telephone, the signs

of her expectancy not yet showing. The call
went through the exchange, where even electricity will stall

as switchboards translate to gossip: by the end of day
the whole town knew and her one call to family

multiplied into dozens of incoming calls
from absolute strangers: 'congratulations, we all

feel your joy . . .'. It's called the telephone paddock:
it's where the line went through. I had to plough 'round
	the poles: a trick

my uncle taught me—setting the discs just right,
following the contours. A retired trucker said he'd got a
    fright

the other day when he heard the tractors no longer
need drivers: can plough a field using GPS—the farmer

can stay at home until his machines run out
of fuel. Weather carries a reciprocity—a bout

of sultry days here seems to mean crisp clear skies
there . . . The lines still burn through crops, and lies

and gossip and home truths hurtle through the exchange.
A birth is something a town will hear about. The range

of opinions on morning sickness will vary
as much as the weather—and humidity

will mean cold days to come before the heat sets in:
a late child will bring on the talk and advice. It's how you
    begin.

OCCASION AT VARIANCE WITH THE WORD

In the corner paddock, four species of birds
        congregate—if not interacting
then scanning spaces between others'
        courses: insect-hunting heron

knifing random lines between scattered
    pink and grey galahs, magpie larks
stressing laws of genre, place, and limits,
    and the crow watching acutely:

caught in heavy pause before flight
    would drag to incident.
In arrangement of data, each bird becomes
    a marker: point or line,

brushstroke outside the picture. Viewed
    from high ground, transferred
to paper, roughly as we see it; at variance
    with records accumulated

across the seasons, those moments
    of pressure and temperature,
agisting light and darkness in the pied
    and variegated image.

THE TOP BUSH

for the Cribbs

The aggregate of words is not enough
to fill in gaps between wandoo trees,
the top bush now entirely bereft
of scrub, termite mounds the rough

end of the stick, the signing off.
In the dry part of day it's hard
to imagine early morning mists in a scarred
and overgrazed under-story, filled out

with the fabrications of vapour.
You can illustrate space, pour
scenarios and simulations into its fabric.
In the canopy, thinned and disconnected,

parrots suggest other inscriptions.
At night, small animals move high up there
and nests in hollows are infra-red, sear
with body-warmth. Bees spill from a storm-torn

wandoo, intense in the coldest month.

POLLEN

As dust to the cuffs of trousers,
puff, atomise; black-cored planets
launching yellow satellites,
as trailing through uninhabited pasture:
wild oats, daisies, Salvation Jane, lupin flowers.
This body, a carry-all, a vehicle for reform;
anarchic pollination in the hungry appetite
of trails heading out from home;
this annual inculcation, infusing
histamine, voltage that alters

the structure of cells . . .
and so I leave again
and wash away the quarantine
the segregation
these writers of history who'd have all settlers
feel comfortable with pollen on the cuffs of trousers,
   identikit
as red around the eyes, these inflammations, these
   referendums—
furiously bright in the spring sunshine,
striking up discussions, confident as bees
almost stalling, but breaking
away—laden—just in time,
our instinctive, driven
representatives.

A VERSION OF THE NEW ARCADIA

Chaff blocks spread and decompose
over summer, autumn, into winter;
reseeding selves, adjusted slightly
to the area, like sentimentality.

Remember. Red-capped robins appeared
on seeding mounts of broccoli,
the reserve filled with jam tree
sandwiched between allotments;

pink and greys, little corellas,
set in the blooded evening—
we don't realise what we miss,
a swirl of bats, rapid tactics,

buzz and multiply as touchpaper,
night sparks when you see
what you hear only, this dimness,
hairs in ears as wide as membranes

floating in hearsay; the soil
soft with weekend rains
rabbits have tested, not echidnas—
no evidence of nosing,

even in the groundline
of termite-eaten stumps,
quarrelsome, tetchy evening hangers-
on as spread statistics

will never hold up as pure nostalgia,
having laid on scheme water and power
and buried an access road
into the title deed, up close,

to watch and almost block out
the overwhelming flock,
just the insects interrupting
purity of chaos theories

as random as caught is not,
precise acidwork in digestion,

the bats come maybe down
from rifts in the mountain,

where planes fly too close
and fate is either 'one day',
or subsumed in inevitability.
Love to air: gnat, mosquito

flitting we might say drifting
with just enough warmth
left after day, to draw blood
from inside bat, silhouettes

sonic in thin light, until radical
the flock pours in plumes and billowings,
canvas flapping furiously on canvas,
all metaphors and similes

associated with the rapid movement
of water over rocks, reefs,
just the swell conflicted
and yet of the same flesh,

the prominent tree struck
against the mountain—bats
blinded momentarily by destruction
of silence. And this to darken

the house, paddocks,
granite bones of the reserve.

WARNING—SNAKES (REPRISE)

The first day of warm weather snakes will be a threat.

Don't walk in the long grass.
Don't go near the old bikes and pile of tin cans.
Don't walk anywhere without announcing
your coming—make noise, just enough noise
and they'll move away. Listen, that rustling
in the grass, that's one moving away.
How do I know? Because I've seen them
from closer than you'd ever want to be,
so close they've turned round to strike me,
brushing my boots. No, I've never hurt one,
I walk away. They don't recognise the demands
of property, and they won't be bought out.
You complain about mice in the barn?
Leave the snakes alone.

THE BROTHERS:
A MONOLOGIC ECLOGUE

Older Brother

We are twins though technically
I am the elder, coming a few minutes
earlier, though he sat on me in the womb
and has always tried to get the better
of me; note his new house, well, new
by comparison, though it's been
across those railway tracks
for sixty years now. Three
stories, pillars and posts,
a galvanised roof that's replaced
every decade, the gleam
running like quicksilver
down through the gutters.

Younger Brother

It's hard to believe the kernel
of the house our mother
gave birth in is buried under
that mess of concrete and mortar:
a hundred-year-old stone house
that looks like a brothel in Tijuana.

Do they have palms in Tijuana?
If they do, then his place
belongs there. Sure it gets
hot enough here, but it's
trying to be somewhere else.
Maybe a sailor's dive
in the tropics: not this dusty
inland place he just won't leave.

Older Brother

He had to set up opposite me:
couldn't go his own way,
find his own place. He got
Dad's money—got the farm
and sold it off. If Mum hadn't
thought of me I'd be nowhere,
but her family always had more dough
than the old man, selfish brute
he was. Two of a kind.
Peas in a pod. He had to set up
opposite me, across the railway line.
Even bought the block opposite
so no one could build out his view.
The gossips tell me it's to keep
an eye on his mother's legacy.
What right? She said: it's uncanny,
they're like two peas in a pod.

Younger Brother

That creeper he cleared away
from the window had been there
since we were kids: a lantana
with twists that cored the deep
places we like to keep closed.
It spiked golden whistlers
into the hot airs, sharper
than barbed wire but perfumed
and harmonious. It still flowered
purple in the heat, and our
games and annoyances
moved from one bloom to another
like determined bees.

Older Brother

As I sense the forgetting
creeping up on me, I add
another room: a room
for where I might have gone
had I not felt a need to keep an eye
on him. I see him out in his garden,
the disturbing mixture of fabaceae
and vegetables. I don't know
how he's kept the asparagus
and artichokes going through drought.
They are fair to middling: the old girl
who keeps house for him—I know,

I know she's his concubine—
sells them occasionally at Saturday
market. Friends of friends
have bought them as presents
for me . . . over the years . . . the labels
never change and nor does his handwriting.
The hearts of artichokes in olive oil.
In each room I use a different
colour paint: the seasons
don't repeat themselves.
they change every year
and so does their colour.

Younger Brother

He read too many books
with plates that weren't quite coloured:
touched up. Islands in the pacific,
mountains blank and something paler than white.
He hated the heat, and he stays.
It was hot the last day we spoke to each other
sixty years gone, there was a species
of bird high in the salmon gum
that no longer exists,
and it took fright with the shouts,
blackened like a sunspot: bright and dark.
He looks like a fool, an old fool
hobbling about. Covered the garden
in concrete—those palms sticking out
like a bad night at the picture house.

And women won't go there.
And that says it all.

Older Brother

He's brought in the Ouch Bush
from the kwongan. Orange haloes
that spike. The smiling guard dog.
Flowers are angry, transplanted . . . cajoled.

Younger Brother

My father said you go to that camp
and you won't get back into this house.
He went, and stayed. He came back
when Dad died. Mum said: take it . . . remain.

ACT 2

REFLECTORS: DRIVE 2

There's a car that does this run
called TONSOFUN. Thirty years ago
in the same model car, your father
would sit on a ton, roo bar painted silver
with black electric tape on the curve
of the bar facing the driver,
keeping the glint within limits
when other boundaries
were smashed out of orbit,
dropping the wheels
onto the gravel shoulder,
snapping white posts and reflectors,
red and silver—back then
they were probably jarrah.
Sometimes he'd swing
back 'round, a vicious u-turn
heightened by a crest or a bend,
and go back to collect
a few trophies for the Wonderheat.
He liked a good evening fire;
burning paint—off-white,
yellow, then red, made him
laugh at himself: a bit of a dickhead.
A journey to the beer fridge.
You'd stare as the fumes
went up the flue, reflectors

melting, whispering through
the hiss of combustion:
Shadrach, Meshach, and Abednego.
Stepmother shrinking pullovers
in the washing machine, drying
them on the clotheshoist
by a guilty fire. In your pocket
slugs from a .22 bolt action,
a cheap one with plastic stock
modelled like woodgrain,
tubular magazine for eight shots,
all hollow-points and a litany
of brass, as if from tombs
of warrior kings, weapons of the *Iliad*
in their gleam, like the roo bar,
the shield with the world written,
stars charted in libations
of dull rooblood. Anti-battle.
Working towards non-violence . . . ?
He tells you of the schoolhouse
in the forest, and the lookout tower
where fires were caught for the telegraph,
illumination of numbers, forests
of maths. This bushland we drive
through joins the past, linked
to his ledgers, facts and figures
eaten by slaters and childhood
curiosity, failure of patrimony.
Slowing today, the wind rocking
the car, semi-chilled from south,
haemorrhaging amongst a touchy
canopy of marri and wandoo.

So slow . . . halving your speed
with each kilometre, winding down,
to stop and listen to weather coming in.
Fine leaves of grevillea rustle,
tuning up for something. Here,
almost the driest month in a century.
And then rain on the roof, the metal
of the car an echo chamber, vinyl interior
baffling and dampening sound. Water
lacquers the windscreen and isn't transparent.
It has texture. It is black, inflecting
granite clouds promulgating
overhead. Fading flowers
of winter. Last night, headlights
dropped out completely, out here:
at the exact point where a roo
has been severed by a roo bar.
Its tail has lost all rigidity,
is hooked like a question mark.
Its face, untouched, a fallacy.
It's not uncommon to see
black-faced cuckoo shrikes here,
their faces 'human', bodies
as sleek as any bird's. This is mythology.
It adapts itself. Headlights out, brakes,
off-road uncertainty. Stock still.
Walk in emptiness, absolute darkness,
or flag down a passing car,
risky out here. Evidence scant.
Or the car stripped down to the axles
by first light . . . not even the light
of a farmhouse. Then snap, back on.

Lightning or beacons, phenomena
within the hemispheres of fittings.
Light quenches imploding night,
all turns inwards. What goes out
comes back in tenfold, and we quiver.
The risk of driving, temptation.
We look out and read darkness
as signal fires might attract
the sailor nearing rocks: outcrops,
heat held in, rare—everything is rare—
orchids moving haltingly towards flowering,
some time off, but in process. Fear
is texture of blackness, underlayer,
mirror-image of past drives,
of all locations—it never leaves
us, just compacts in the head.
It's all in the head, behind the face
of the slaughtered roo, nest-hungry
cuckoo-shrike. It's the pigment of sight.
How loud is the kangaroo's suffering?
We can walk but can't drive
in the absence of pictures, pain
a viscous wash spreading over gravel,
compacted dirt. The road is a communicator.
It speaks suffering. The cleared edges
ragged and robbed for firewood,
forays for remnant wildflowers.
Plastic containers linger, a few
hubcaps spinning off and lodging
against a trunk persisting by the road,
reflectors tapped into the skin of a wandoo
to catch a homecoming. Stops you

shooting by and missing it entirely.
Reflectors with contact skew light
and illustrate unexpected places.
They catch nothing directly,
and, we suspect, produce something
like spells or divinations.
They sought me as I sought them,
they beheld us at the appointed time
and place . . . night vapour, car heater
stops, starts, mostly blows air colder
than outside. Food wrappers collect
around particular root systems—
companies advertise and call
names of rebellious houses.
It's a ploy, like light, like the Latin
names for plants that disappear
year by year. The father bought a house
in the country so he could retrace
his journeys every other weekend.
To hang around family vicariously,
family that had divorced him. One half
of him might have annulled darkness,
but the house was elevated and stood out,
bright in sunsets, heavy in gloom.
This lasted years, and when he
searched elsewhere for answers,
he placed it on the market, where it brooded
and soured surrounding paddocks.
Flocks of cockatoos fragmented
up to a line of thought, then stopped
on atoms, never moving further.
Superstition, but already folklore.

Without horizons, every line, fold,
point in the immediate distance
ends something. It's the nature
of gossip. Of red and yellow stickers,
cars over the pits, who knows whom,
registration stickers building
histories on windscreens. That's
how they know you. Nicknames,
pet names—howya goin' pilgrim?
This road, mecca for culture and hidden
crops, unregistered, undeclared,
secretive owners at church singing
to the Robert Juniper stained-glass windows,
cars arranged on the opposite bank
of the Avon, over the swing bridge,
like emblems, discreet, never
overstated, cross-pollinating prayers and hymns,
smiting Delilahs and praising Davids,
adding up profits and scriptures from Monsanto,
healthy body healthy soul healthy nation,
stiffhearted but drooling over new technologies,
twenty-five years of pig farming, each cell
in the shed smaller than when they began,
and the pigs fatter. The small genitals
on their youngest son can be boosted
up with an injection—see what it does
for piglets. And horse-floats sail
like yachts from Royal Perth
or Freshwater Bay yacht clubs
up and down the Swan River,
twilight sailing on a weekday evening,
toasting Perth theatre and new cars. Horse-floats

sail like fibreglass or wooden-hulled boats
with jibe-sail full, but never intense.
The spinnaker unfurls on the open roads.
They flow like Range Rovers
or Jeep Cherokees, carrying
cargoes of fine blood
shaped like horses.

CLEARING THE DEAD LONG GRASS

It had to be the mad mower
who dobbed us in, our sanctuary
encircled by firebreaks, the heady lupins
branching out, the wild oats lashing
the sea-breeze that eventually
makes its way in; I don't need to be there
to picture the scene: Stephen and John
out there with whipper snipper,
Katherine only partially covered
by Sun Block, gathering
like a scene from Pushkin,
or any number of peasants
reprised from in situ painting;
I can hear the Bartok,
I can hear the Sculthorpe,
the gathering of the sheaves,
the trailer piled high
in the muggy pre-storm air;
it had to be the mad mower

who dobbed us in; he watched
it from his spray pod, his ride-on-mower;
he crossed the fenceline and spray-seeded
and Roundup'd the fire risk in the middle
of the green season (yes, I harp on,
like a broken record, a one-trick pony) ;
I yearn to return, to return so I can be angry,
get a bee in my bonnet,
something stuck in my craw,
to labour only half-willingly
under a sun that will tear
into the exposed skin like fire.

FROM QUALANDARY CROSSING TO YENYENNING LAKES: A PASTORAL

Navigable, this facility,
all volume and quality
in the deadzone, anatomical
on false shores, circles
into a frozen core,
salt that burns like the tail
of a comet, ridges and gates
controlling inflow,
outing heavy water
that's a vehicle for exposure,
poseur, exhibit: vehicle
for misgivings that cipher nature
inwards; maybe this is why

poison gathers between sign posts,
spiked by stream gauge stations
measuring illusory qualities
of surface and interior,
liquid body we cling to;
sheoak and melaleuca,
scarified by wind,
huddle over white banks,
blanks of scalding and chemical process,
mulga parrots and twenty-eights,
greenfields simmering up
from the brim of lakes
baked and blasted with 'the terror',
'the menace', the dammed crossing;
steel-gated spreadsheet
wall of fundamentalist
recreationalism, leverage
and social skills refuged
in the gauges, keeping it in-house,
within region and over-explanation
ruining psychology, we like
to be left hanging, time
inevitably ending, that'd cut
the outside world in half,
then half again, and so on
until time can't be folded. Angles—blue,
inviting—fields of superphosphate
denying channels carved
ridge or plateaus low layered
strata or sub-drift of colourants,
soil types fused and enhancing
floodways as families gloat

over barbecues on pristine sand
that's strange to touch, almost surreal, as if it should
be mined and turned into the skin
of a military aircraft, powerboats
droning through low-water, churning up,
kind of tacky and sticky,
prop furrows held in place
for that split second, semi-solid
like the flesh of saltbush,
moebius branches vascular
against tepid blue winter skies, partial drought
honed in flaking skins of peripheral
melaleucas, in hijinks
of a drifting telegraph pole—
history frosted at the base: spark, tow, quench,
shin-high crops lurid green
on rising ground, palming
burial mounds or in the least
taboo and hexing and unfleshly
life-forces, ag department
and its craving for profits,
mining company shining
drift of peeled back forests
further south, and caveat emptor,
danger—amoebic meningitis,
increasing as water warms and observers
on ski-boats 'do the right thing';
special effects, life-parodies
carved with violence, fired and sharpened
against a depressed horizon,
black-winged stilts' leg-like elements
heating shallows, corrie iron shelters

taut and uncomfortable with sudden gusts,
trunks beyond white, stressed to the point
of impact: absorbing reflections
of an animate self; tracks
of four-wheel drive vehicles
compelling poachers,
compelling blood
in the developing solution.

AGAINST CONFLATION

Designed to keep the parrots out
the Nissen hut of netting
trapped a pair of twenty-eights
vingt-huit, vingt-huit, vingt-huit,

a French colony, historic,
like the closing of brothels in Roe Street
or the surveillance
and vigilantes in Smith Street—

the new phoneboxes without
glass walls, citizens
with clipboard hoping
for kerb-crawlers, spitting

at streetwalkers—of refined varieties
in gardens that won't tolerate
trampling, the 'wandering about',
roughing it on the edge

of salinity, or in lingo,
making a go of it,
despite the gentrification,
the naming, the lists

bred from a new mathematics.
A storm struck hard
in the summer, and that's why
the netting lifted. The parrots'

panopticon of colours
looking for an out—
extra-spectra, safe in the open,
the daylight, their language.

WHITE COCKATOOS

Spectres inverting sunlit
paddocks after late rain
field into quadrature out

of blind-spots, raucous
it's said, like broken glass
in a nature reserve

but that's no comparison;
cowslip orchids' yellow parameters
curl like tin, or cowslip orchids'

yellow parameters reflect clusters
of white feathers from canopies
of wandoos or sheaths of flight,

down in deep green crops
ready to turn when rains are gone,
beaks turned back towards

whereabouts unknown,
but almost certain to appear,
at least as atmosphere.

WHITE-FACED HERON

The white-faced heron seems grammar and action
as the sun sharpens poise and balance,
solitary in a field provokes a reaction.

Clots and twists of cloud confuse the fraction,
divisible quantity of math and trance,
the white-faced heron seems grammar and action.

The surety of her being creates an equation,
dawn and sunset trigger clairvoyance,
solitary in a field provokes a reaction.

We invest ourselves in her volatile station,
formulate moods on the fact of her presence,
the white-faced heron seems grammar and action.

It's the pattern of speech we define as tension,
the hope of her being there, the thrill of chance,
solitary in a field provokes a reaction.

Language shapes a waterbird's intention,
pasture and water shape her stance,
the white-faced heron seems grammar and action,
solitary in a field provokes a reaction.

AN OCCASION TO CONFIRM AGAIN . . .

The rufous songlark just is, in the rain;
a dry winter dissolves into a wet spring
and the seams unweld again;
volcanic soil cracks and infuses seed,
catalytic and virulent over the rising
water table; stray mallee firmly anchored

not picking up the wind, wrapped around
granite; in time, laws and defamations
fire and haze, subdivisions
pushed through Council with its new Shire President,
then closed again. To fold time
over renewal, challenge punctuation, as slow

on firebreaks the tractor ambles, spraying
euphemisms, weeds suppressed as towns
or emblems; they say we love
we say as atoms or bonds of inhalation, dust

masks just ritual, good vibes for patrons. Garden
windhovers, and below the songlark

ambivalent at the joins, this distraction
we breathe again, leaves sharp as occasional
quotations, arising dialect of brightness.

SILVER-EYES

Silver-eyes annul fruit
of variety
and phraseology
so rapidly nothing
gets through this taut wiring,
the soft flesh of stone fruit,
in jam tree and York gum
georgic intensity—
a cumulative sound rips
air space, locality,
as declared pests outflank
like consciousness, avert
blank laws of property.

SWALLOW

Delta arrow, transmission
call-up, ID rapid, sharp, revolutionary
prompting, outer through inner
exposition in the English novel,
as if wildcard, chemical excitability,
stray configuration that's never random,
as between figures
they'll chance, and up-eaves
build staggering nestings, or suspend
against conditions; at school
it was rumoured one impaled itself
in a student's leg—suburban myth
or likely story, protest
and radical exaltation.

EAGLE

Seen briefly over Wallaby Hills
it distorts the way we witness
errors in a fenceline, patches
where sheoaks work the southerly
outside science. Immense,
it stabilises before going

with the currents, making cold air
productive, and small animals
carrion on our event
horizon. Hakeas fibrillate
and charges of stamens fall
in brushes, yellow magnetic,
wires charging up to the heavyweight:
uplifted overhead.

WILLY WAGTAIL

Tacked down pat by heavy rain
a twitching tail absorbs refrains
of late season, and wheat ears

filling out to flesh the fields
bedraggled, purple flowers
suppressed and crushed

limply to their centres; but
the puff of a tiny chest
alert to pressure, switches

and swivels surveillance,
the sun behind the clouds
mirrored in its actions,

ungreyed by shelter,
its quick reaction
to imitation: we step out

chilled by reservations,
keen to shed our syllables, call
its actions models of behaviour.

CONSPIRACY

Blame takes the gravel road, the impact, a boobook owl
caught in early morning semi-blind swoop
from wandoo to wandoo, hollow-limbed nesting trees
removed as roads widen, transport to dry areas expands.
Making the desert grow the useless growth goes.
So they say. Conspiracy is no theory,
and what you see is what you get.
Prayers for the crow pecked to death by chickens
killed by a fox nights later, the rooster elevated
to hero, though he perished too. In stripping away
terms of reference, we're still hot,
the pool bringing little comfort, stunning sunsets
running like chemicals through memory.
Unable to categorize, the circuit breaks
and lightning does strike up
conversations, verbal antics in the tin shed,
a jagged scar of runoff—overflow of rainwater.
Birds forced to fly in another district come here
like registers, digitalised now, the true borders
as once claimed lost, blown out. The quarry owner
knocked off fifty hectares of virgin bushland
without clearance, which might have come anyway.
The fines aren't massive, and new suburbs

down the freeway will house families
where maybe one child out of five hundred
will protest to preserve the infinitesimally small
remainder of forest when he or she learns to distrust,
even hate, the shape of the stone the house
is made from. The suffering of birds
alters perspective. Bird-death knocks out
clauses of light. Those dark patches—floaters—
they swim the eye. Dead birds trying to fly.

ELEGANT PARROTS/WAL-BYNE

Please,
in this unleavened light,
this pair compose
no analogue
tempered by rock-chips,
branches
washed and dried,
trees exculpated from species,
cured as the flock imprints,
light inside the body
needs no unlocking;
a month or two they separate
in mating, slight difference
in heat and typeface:
expelled, you find your way
here, traipse
the concordance,

template without friction.
Unripe seed
is still green on white waste,
saline-drop like vespers,
that time of day
at odds, ribboned orange and indigo,
hand-squeezed
drawn to extremities: filtered, diluted, worn down:
this enchanted crypt of quartz,
small enough to be forgotten,
taken away.

ANOTHER WAY OF SEEING A RED-CAPPED ROBIN

Female redback spider
in full egg-laying regalia,
clasped to the head
of an anonymous bird,
its chest torn by wire
or burning from a ravaged heart,
perched on the outer tip
of a desolate tree,
nameless and uncertain.

TWENTY-EIGHT PARROT DOUBLE SONNET HYMN AND EULOGY

A sine curve along the axis
of fenceline, digressing
in camber and swerve, praxis
past sheep dams, suffocating
skin on water near sticky
floors, to shadow or louder
still, declare companionship
collaborative, hot easterly
roaring to cut yellow and worship
green splays, bursts of powder-
bark, silvered leaves, nexus
of kids on a motorbike racing
silhouettes, throttle and skedaddle
beyond ring-necks' side-saddle.

They hang about, bright sparks
as kids would have it: skylark
around, as chronometers
wound against the shifting waters
of green paddock or paddock
stripped back to ash and rock;
dropping cumquat and plum
they rouse the farmer's gun
and the malicious ones who poison
wheat and watch as the flock

chokes on tongues, sun
half out of their eyes, the sum
of their colour running into cracks
opened in sky and syntax.

ON NOT SEEING THE CRESTED BELLBIRD AT DUCK POOL RESERVE, MORTLOCK RIVER: A GRAPHOLOGIA

The fantail by the {tree [dropped
over the trail]}, sandy soil
holdall for the grim Mortlock's
hydraulics eaten out,
                          a rusty drool
or special sort of tannin,
pelt-banks of not-quite luminous grass
fantail analogy: that trail blocked
by dropped tree, the chatter
this far from the main road . . .
                              dumped wire,
melt-down plastic of herbicide containers,
shotgun cartridges and the litany of bones,
salty interiors paralleling fenceline—
choked—
              a crest of sheoaks and miniature conifers,
the latent Christmas tree wired by mistletoe.
                              The radio crackles
and bigots miss their opportunities
in reserves of euphoria,

locals treating
subtexts as their own,
pink-ribboning
and listening hard to bellbirds
altering sounds in the anatomy of mallee,
cryptograms we'll never decode.

EXCHANGE—VIT. D HUNGER

Because I don't live through summers
every strand of sunlight is absorbed
and collected; the intricate
workings of bees, tactile
and tenacious movements of thornbills
registered, locked up outside electrodes

and X-rays, and garbled in nightmares
or under hypnosis; what's not taken, a chemical
pattern that through heat and reaction
will be changed, will make something
else out of the spectrum. If this is prayer,
then winter warmth and an air marred

only by floating tissue and the cold static
of unremembered strings and sequences
drive it inside out, an exchange
of colour, blood sprayed
into the spectrograph, that no pollution can entirely
obscure. The formula: the wing, the prayer.

THE TASK: DISTRACTION AND HAWK

When the hawk isn't hunting
there is no hook in its beak
and the air isn't serrated,
edges not whetted and a gleam
in striations of winter sunlight
sharpen nothing. It's bone
and cartilage, claws curled
inwards. But in the same passing,
if we imagine ourselves out of sight,
or fragmented between purposes,
glimpsing and forgetting, corner
of the eye, or distracted
by a task, the rapid silence,
a sullenness that makes you wary
and moody, conflicted and uncomfortable,
or fascinated without unity—
the vacuum drawing small birds
and their song into its intention,
vanishings and visibility
as pronounced as a shadow
as if gliding and hovering
are not pleasures enough,
or pleasure is a register
of the leisured and devout.

ROADKILL SHOCK ROCKS THE GALAH'S WORLD . . .

'I spiritualogic grin, in.'
—BAD BRAINS

Roadkill shock rocks the pink and grey's
galah world, this is not wordplay, or deathpuns,
until the sun goes down, shocker, blood-letter,
hit and run make-over, splatterfest and gore show,
a 'laugh-a minute' partner wandering about in a daze,
follow-up slaughter wagons near missing,
hey, arseholes, enjoy the lingua thrill, make it franca,
the spinal cord-charged shadows of York gums
fracturing over the road, a moment's pause
with the colour of it: so pink in the sun . . .
and the decorative compatibility of grey and blood,
the angles warped and fractal, the spilled grain
it was feeding on arranged in a supercilious grin:
at a loss, this companion bird, staggering rear window.

THE CULL

The town is culling
Corellas—they sing
   Too loud, shred the trees
Always gathering
Along the river, ring
   On ring of Dante's

Hell-hole. So, it frees
The townies' souls—frees
   Their sleep of limp dreams.
Early morning chorus
Prayers of broken glass,
   Apart at the seams.

Now, twelve-gauge shot streams
Through the birds, blood steams
   Like river slurry,
A little girl screams
And her mother deems
   It necessary.

The dead—contrary
To dark clouds—hurry
   Over the windrows
Lightly. A starry
Night marks their story.
   White noise follows.

THE MULGA-EUCALYPT LINE

Where semi-arid meets arid,
arid meets semi-arid,
the purple-crowned lorikeet—
red lores blazing, volta
between black hook
of seed-hacking beak,
purple hemisphere
ellipses—ups
the ante of a speech
we can't mimic.
Crossing the mulga-
eucalypt line
the bus kicks up feathers
on a mirage-ridden
road,
so hot to those
just beyond their limit,
just out of reach.

ECLOGUE OF THE BIRDS

Twenty-Eight Parrot

Bold as brass the nip and tuck,
elevation and descent, sweeping strokes
of the sign-off, I stake a claim
and humour myself; though laughter
is what you'd call it, I know it as something else.
These light funnels, tunnels of irregular
nesting trees, hollowed-out flight-lines,
the scratchings on seed membranes
some might see as veins, this blood
of the shoot, dead under
rose hips and wattle blooms.

Magpie

Hair tuft, scalp patch, the bigger they come . . .
the sun gets us going, volatile as nesting season,
never gloating—that's all propaganda,
high or low in wandoo or salmon gum,
deflecting seasonal inflections off the grey
of our razor-sharp beak, to beg
by comparison, lexicographers
of the flyers, though always local,
particular in our heights. Who speaks

for the speared insect, the locusts
pierced through, examined
against the plenty of plague.
They shoot parrots, not magpies!

Twenty-Eight Parrot

That colourful can be haunting
is quelled in rebel compatriots,
to flock or twist in couplets,
stutter across the grotty branches,
drop honkey nuts in bundles
scoured like glacial pickings
when this place was somewhere
other; they drill below us for water,
yelling an approximation
of a name neither attracts
nor damns us. Sedentary
is not our nature, we fly
to avoid early dismissal.
This is no place for the worker.
We make the flashiest targets.

Magpie

Leisure? Offensive. We prised
the akubra and homburg
from the head of a codger,
who thinks himself suited
to walks of pleasure.

The give of sinews,
eye-glint enhanced
by blood—wherever
they come from . . . they nationalise
their fear. Proprietary,
they compensate with clear-felling,
nest-fall in the clipped tongue
of progress, catch-phrase
that'd sell us to the zoo. Free
to come and go, icons
re-naturalised as military budget.

Twenty-Eight Parrot

Blow blue cheeks and yellow belly,
neck the neck of your frivolous lover,
ring around the binary, green-winged
and streaked blue, consorting regally;
this fire we set, these trees we ingratiate
so illustratively as they drive home
against the light, the sun dazzling
and memory that predictable,
or inverting it, what we are
is what they hope we'd be,
glimpses and renderings,
'Port Lincolns' they'd have us
just wandering a little North
of the Stirlings, walking the line,
night-flying when we should be settled.

Magpie

Body blow, torn ligaments, battle-scarred.
In others' myths we speak, and speak out
our own blood-lines, as brother
to sister, offspring to mother
and father—vocative warblings,
emphasis on xenophobia . . . ?
Playthings of the media?
They feed on us. Charcutiers!

⬦⬦⬦⬦⬦ **ACT 3** ⬦⬦⬦⬦⬦

REFLECTORS: DRIVE 3

Moonlight hides more
than it reveals, intensifying
shadows, bold and emphatic
in the core of objects,
but diffuse as double imaging
on the outer, haze and blue
cogitate, and a turn-off
is over-driven slightly;
quick early frost bites back,
third coldest night recorded
in the State: referred sunlight,
imagined it's more painful,
a cascading of the soul,
damaged dashboard jagging
light, vinyl and metal and glass
and recall of a fetish swinging
from the mirror, a sequence
from the car's previous
owner's memory? Transfer
papers bring accountability,
low beam spreading like fog lights,
chain reacting with moonlight.
Single strands in the cubed haystack—
industrial, modular, apartment block—
shine sharply, strands of silver wire,
burning through particles of darkness

no bigger than sand, swept up by a windstorm
you can't feel—silhouettes of trees
cardboard, perfectly still, like single
frames of a movie, or shadow puppets
resting up at the Tintookies Show
at the Fremantle Town Hall
in early primary school,
early 70s nationalism,
only telling part of the story.
Aboriginal myths happened
in other parts of Australia,
along with billabongs. Teachers
denied the veracity of gnamma holes.
Like religious education: watching
Catholics being led outside;
it was all about darkness and light,
the moon problematic . . . sensuous?
A suppression of stars, glowering
predations of owls and tawny frogmouths,
sharp teeth of native cats—rarely
seen or spoken about, cautious
and rapid rodents, cybernetic
interstices of animal, plant, and flakes
exfoliated from granite, hard surfaces
all exterior, old ranges run down
to gentle rises beyond dip and crest,
booby traps—a fence continuing
where the texture of wire
changes, fine light rusting out
to dullness then blankness, trip!
The walking out you do as every
five kilometres a sign times you home,

low-ground salinity edging
out from luminescent creeks,
tidal movements a shattered flow,
a rippling out to limits
of pulse or echo, a place
where bread and flesh
are one and the same thing,
out-manoeuvring interlocution,
ranks of angels or icons,
weird stories and neo-realisms.
Therein the dialectic of social struggle.
Therein hunger and greed.
Therein avarice and sterility.
Diverging from the exact route,
nearing the mountain, jam trees plume
and flight paths prevaricate,
red pulse tagging columns of black light,
shadow-spouts fuming to points
beyond the moon. Across the track
of the car, ten minutes back, a woylie,
'miniature kangaroo', propelled
towards the wandoo of Wambyn Reserve,
beyond the lunar reflector.
In this culture the machine
peaks at night. Fuelling at The Lakes
you're near a pack of drivers
of slaughter trucks—four lined up,
their noses towards the abattoirs
of the South; they don't usually stop
loaded, so something's up—the moon
up strong and bright, their language
fast with coffee and sleep deprivation:

'Down in Katanning there's a mob
of Muslims cut up their own meat.
Halal killing. They keep their women
clean as well—cutting out their bits,
clits, lips, and all!' Muffled laughter
vanished to the sounds of the bowsers,
the group offence so deep.
'Sick fucking bastards', before
an older driver brought closure:
'That's a little bit steep . . .', the sheep
bleating, layer on layer. The names
on their trucks synergistic,
euphemisms for rape and pillage.
The machine moves out among
a range and phase of colourations,
informants of light and dark:
there being no black and white.
Bands of violet shoot the ledges—
blue varies in shades and purple
indulges indigo; light makes fallacies
of the solid, we move in its headlights.
Light is the prayer's substance,
it collates shifts, inhabits. It changes
appearance—now a burning green
along the ridge, more dense
than the black core of the mountain.
Clouds block the moon—it effuses,
winces, is enveloped. Pitched into,
pupils great circles, at full tilt
we increase: fear, rapid breathing,
skin tight as . . . land and clouds
translate, and you become the conduit,

movement and vinyl inadequate
insulation, if insulation at all.
The radio breaking up doesn't
distract you. Static more organised
than music. It possess a wave language,
the car decelerating into looping curves,
double white lines thickening and growing
harder, a dull buzz in the stomach
spreading out. The vanquishing becomes sexual.
God inhabiting your body you realise
the reflectors have connected. Lit up.
You verge in faith, in ecstasy,
towards an accident. Rapture
a split moment and the woylie appearing
and your sense kicking back in!
Clear nights activate wildlife.
Danger clarifies dusk and dawn.
Manifold and surprising.
Real estate. Realty. Plot of land.
Title deed. The place that abuts Wambyn
ignites with the moon. The For Sale
sign visible, though the text
dark and impenetrable.
To the city traveller fantasising
a leisurely countrification,
it might read, Mistah Kurtz—he dead.
You plan a visit in daylight,
moon impressing itself,
scorching the old growth of grass trees,
stirring up sheoaks. An old commune:
sheds, smashed asbestos sheeting,
rusting playground equipment,

a bunch of barbecues, scattered plastic chairs,
rotting mattresses, flailing powerlines,
a deep dam unholy in its mesmerism,
sparse wandoo, salt. The creeks
really scars, run-off from the neighbouring
property cutting it up, crystals
and New Age sensibilities
shot to pieces, sheep trucks
racketing past over and over,
putting paid to the utopian dream,
vision of one-ness, single male guru
sexing his females, free and 'liberated',
caught between farmer and road,
on the fringe of the woylie's
diminishing territory. Mantra,
mandala, circles stretching out
from the moon, deracinating
as a carload of bigots motors past,
replete with a weekend at the York rally:
look, by light of day it's a piece of shit.
Not much of a weekend retreat.
They change the subject,
concentrating on stud bulls and City Beach,
the 'war' with Boat People
and Australia's domination of the cricket,
making, in their own way, dark eclogues.

ARCADIA AGONISTES

The rain, soundless, is crimson
on third beats, the eucalyptus leaves
brought in dry for lightloss,
river gum stacked against a wall
is its own world shaped, stacked
orderly, paths crossing or closed off
or isolated under prisings of bark,
webs in knots, saliva-pasted soil
crumbling in seams while termites adjust
in hearts, or cores stretching as far
as the saw allowed, segmented cellular
compaction, this ground gone over,
and burnt to a fine ash, ciphered
in another similar-looking piece
with similarly motivated or dormant
termites; the point being they all burn
no matter how much you shake the wood
or lift the bark, the creatures
we don't see. The mutated virus
doesn't live, so life hasn't been created?
Anomalous plants holdfast and saturate,
dry beneath the skin, float comedies
and tragic interludes that require
no agency, the wind testing the flue,
ashbed chemical and altering mood
and structure as the block on the corner—

for sale—might be discussed with reticence
or dramatic impetus. The wood brought
from out on Quairading Road—within the district—
flourished on a different soil type, rainfall
slightly less despite the creek
and it being less than twenty
minutes' drive if abiding
by the speed limit. Brought here
to be burnt, to be made ash
for the garden. Heat feeds on reactions
increasingly complex, fuel becomes scarce.
All logical as hormones and the need
multiplying while fires become silent
as rain—less colourful—
inflamed by drought.

CROP DUSTER

It is the noun behind the action
that wrecks the choral work,
stiff breeze across drought-tweaked
ears of wheat charged with late rains,
aerofoils catching and sweeping
aquatic, harmonic exhalations
of scrub and pathways
that survey undulations; for here
the crop duster, sharp single-seater
with gull wings displaying,
ballet parody, stench of poison

imposing the shadow of a suppressive
kiss: Cape Tulip a legacy
on uncropped surface,
serial movements of emblematic parrots
escorting, switching at low-level
transfer stations, to bind the journey;
crop duster, aerial sprayer, farm-acology
mapped in the iris, as if seeing clouds
of spray billow out will necessarily
suggest a bitter odour, ingestion,
despite the wind blowing
in the opposite direction,
and we in our porous skins,
moving fast and further away.

BREAKING THE BONDS

The blunt axe recoils off the dense
cylinder—tight-skinned, dead, and dry
though its moist signature locked
in every cell. Swinging again, it jams
askew, a jagged incision, twisted imprint.
Caught at cross-purposes, prising molecules
apart, intensified by the circular saw,
singing revolutions, belt from tractor
flapping like celluloid shot on Super-8
movie cameras—those uncertain
movements of childhood transferred
to video and disk now, a forest

full of wood, a father in awe
of his father, but grandson perplexed
by impact, axe sharp through flickering
decay, gigantic strand of hair on the screen,
vibrating like a cheap special effect,
inducing fear. The axe chips and slowly
bites wood, sinews, and ligaments
snapping and drawing attention
to themselves, as over and over
the same spot is struck, and grain
gives way, solid broken into smaller
parts, grown dead beneath the bark.

ANOTHER DROUGHT YEAR . . .

The front disdains and the white-faced heron
wears a pained expression, cantilever on brittle
limb of dead tree by the shed. The wind shifts—
it buckles wire legs, and twists, eye gyroscopic
on its grammatical neck, an accent from an unfamiliar
language. There is no original thought or unique
observation, just repetition, the refrain
that overwhelms the lyric; too many melody lines
straining from shadehouse fabric, dysfunctional
equipment being stripped and plundered for spare parts,
acacias that maintained a foothold when clearing
and subdivision interrupted, severed the tracks.
New growth bright with yellow bloom
resists and sounds in a tautological sense.

The rain gauge shows a couple of points—
there'll be no more in this crossing over
and the white-faced heron makes this clear.

CHANGING THE FENCELINE

The feed reduced, the course of a wire river
is diverted, striations twisted and reset, at odds
with light which is cooled by dark but hollow
cloud; rescue-sheep force the fence, rainless
pasture low in any case, hunger failing
to neutralise the poison of Cape Tulip—
ample quills mocking drought, making
their own water out of stale breath,
sucking up space, stimulated by hooves.
It's the Devil's place, as the banks size up.

So the fenceline moves, ups-stakes and heads off—
star pickets unearthed, transplanted, reset,
interlock mesh swinging in deep arcs—
an array that might detect a pulsar—
tracking another chart. Close to the house now,
sheep, wire. Saplings, no longer
protected from sheep, glow
as green as feed—dry lupins and oats
not enough, the light grass rapidly cleared.

In changing coordinates the leading wether
eyes the doorway of the house—sanctuary,

micro-climate, eater of light? The fires burn fiercely,
wood—combustible dust, but water flows
freely, and green feed is had at a price.

GOING TO SEED: ENJAMBED

for John Tranter

Obliged being here, these threads
that garment crops and conversations,
the pipes that carry refreshment and waste,
bales of chaff and hay that sprout wheat
and the odd tuft of oats, yellow bricks
greening about the gills, but lively
and enthusiastic with emergence, only
to dwindle through lack of nutrients, seedy
but never going to seed, tang of germination
a lush sermon in a cold church, faith
and warmth indirectly proportional,
then directly proportional, then unrelated,
as if belief is climatic. Bales rot
with more rain and a different, gangrenous
green takes over, white tentacles of sun-starved
weed-stalks . . . roots becoming roots . . . trailing
out to greylight, delicate but in turmoil
over pigment, reconstructing from a different stem,
life beginning as if delayed, or the slow reaction
of sedation, gradually breaking down in the soil
of flesh, the sap a blood-type found in prayer

caught mid-air, reaching out and hoping
systole, diastole, a bed of hay as blond
as hair and skin of the boy on the poster
from Wagin—displayed in the Terrace,
city business district, heart and soul
of the State's fortunes, innocence
of a small Grecian god, Hobbytex smile—
if the brand's still relevant to this generation—
cast from leftover stock in wheatbelt Wagin
from before the War—any war.

SCYTHE

Long-handled grass cutter, protractor, swinger on the
    hooked
shoulder, the bent elbow, the outspoken handles
nothing on the blade misnomering through grass—
more resistant than might be assumed,
in tender or sharp narratives,
to ward off prosecution, the hypocrites
hiding from the cause of riots,
to scintillate in grass, dead beyond the roots.
You pick up one of these at an auction,
to cut through depression—all low down in its action,
the risk is barely the ankles, though drop
in swathes it does, in this oppressive heat,
lubricity and clouds amplified over the mountain—
to sharpen the grammatical curve is the skill,
the way the arc increases, gets faster, like increments

in a guitar riff at an angry concert, but in slicing
don't go near the jam tree sapling, don't go near
the jam tree cutting—these planes of the paranormal,
of stand-up comedy, the bats that fly over here at night
we never see precisely; let's collect severed grass,
make sheaves and ricks, stack them like small gods
of local order; in real time the clouds build grey, even
   black,
heavy along the eroded crest of the Dyott Range: they
   whet
the sickle, invert the spark as struck against a granite
boulder the district might draw its breath in: every day
is the same, and none of us thinks about it. The risk
drives and we call it produce, the storm might strike
and cremate; so swing high, swing low, the sun is hidden
from sight, the prism of the scything makes our bones
ache: the twitch that does for a forecast—here
grasshoppers flying on ahead.

WHIPPER SNIPPER

Whipper snipper, brush cutter, line trimmer,
wild oats dropped in swathes, plastic wire
chewing trees down near the roots, rocks
and fencewire fighting back: the cutting
of the long grass—Shire-declared fire risk—
is violence either way you look at it.
Whipper snipper, brush cutter, line trimmer.

Whipper snipper, brush cutter, line trimmer,
the incessant buzz, the guttural rev when in the thick
of it, spinning wildly—so fast wild is really wild—
when the cutter flies off. Revving out, oat dust,
cells of paper, lung lining, casting a pall
through Polaroid safety glasses—into dusk,
the sun a blue grey colour, like the corona
of an other-worldly fire. The scream of tear and rip,
louder than a thousand corellas, louder than the motor.
Whipper snipper, brush cutter, line trimmer.

Whipper snipper, brush cutter, line trimmer,
out in the arc of the electric scythe,
electric death march; first day out maybe the heat,
the dust, but the murder of a cricketer weighed
on my mind. So many people violent at the moment
a swatch of yellow-gold oats drops, their seedcases
long emptied and lighter than air, swirling
in the heat. And I think of the jam tree saplings
I skirt around, resisting the flight of moths,
the moving away of snakes at least warned by the hell
of a din; the second day out I was astonished
at each changeover—cutter, fuel, cleaning of the spark
    plug—
that I recalled nothing, recalled thinking nothing at all.
Whipper snipper, brush cutter, line trimmer.

FIRESTORM

The community bearing up, the weight of two deaths,
twelve thousand hectares burnt to the ground,
running through late-harvest crops
ready to fall into the mouth of the header,
rolling flames and junkets of smoke,
the whiplash eucalypt torch-bearer
hot winds wrecking the area, taking all
with them; so close to the dam,
so close to the cold waters,
caught in the spirals of the firestorm;
to cross the road, to cross shires,
while those who survive would say:
'no sightseers', or 'what's left worth preserving?'
The heat letting nothing grow back.

LOCATION

Out of the crop a pair of kangaroos:
through fence and into the reserve.
Sundew and cowslip orchids make us complex
and sanguine in late afternoon. Our daughter
wants to tell the sighting for news at school,
but we warn her to keep the location secure—

the fathers of boys who hassle her
taking them out shooting, such information
sure to lead to phone calls then spotlights
in paddocks, death of wildflowers
in the reserve. It's a close-knit community,
and management of fragmentary
bush is nominal, fences down
and sheep wandering in for extra feed,
rabbit traps along sandy tracks,
despite rare visits due to a lack
      of barbecues.

VISTA OVERLOAD: TRAVERSING ATMOSPHERICS

On returning: chaff dust
of firebreaks, slashed down
lupin testament, second-year saplings
green and growing without water,
the ground rock-hard; fire impact
in the Mortlock, broom myrtle stands
and corvid allusions sounded, to rail against
the spotter plane, sucker action
imprinted as the kitchen run-off
fuels ante-seasonal faction; to say Hamlet
is the case for action, I come back,
loosen over the apron below mountain
and antennae, concupiscent in the bedroom
half-shaded from the sun, or burning moonlight;

and the fox angry amongst dryandra,
dogs packing it up the road,
our prospects hydroponic,
it being that dry, that forewarning
of a heat that'll drop us, sort us out;
in the good books the snakes don't strike at night,
the machinery that thrives hard in the dark
keeps us cool, tampers with the atmosphere,
frustrates the blowflies.

ECLOGUE OF PRESENCE

'Ye goatherd gods, that love the grassy mountains'
—PHILIP SIDNEY
'. . . a community of thieves . . .'
—XAVIER HERBERT

Farmer

Everything you see stretched between river and hills
is mine, and you need my permission to cross even the
    gullies
that run along the fenceline—I've seen you hanging
    around in the scrub,
looking the place over—well, I'll warn you, I hear a noise
and shoot first . . . you think being up so early in the
    morning
will keep me from knowing, think again—and my eyes see
    into the evening.

Young Bloke

This scrub is for anyone to walk through, unna? And when
   evening
comes we don't hang around anyway, there's spirits that
   come out of the hills
that'll get even a bloke like you. In the early morning
we come from town to watch the roos leap the gullies
and escape from your farm before machine-noise
makes them afraid, before they vanish into the scrub.

Farmer

If a kangaroo has a go at my crops and takes to the scrub
I'll go straight after it, or wait until evening
where I'll catch it on a trail with a spotlight, and the noise
they hear will be the sound of death come down from the
   hills,
down from my house where guns are loaded, no gullies
will protect them, and they'll never see morning.

Young Bloke

My dad says your family brought mourning
to my cousins, unna? And though the mallee scrub
hides your killing, and though the gullies
are choked silent with wire and sheep carcasses, evening
brings a light that shows the dead the way up to the hills
where they fill the darkness and occupy every noise.

Farmer

I've a good mind to give you a hiding and shut that noise
that's spewing out of your mouth; the only mourning
that'll be known around here is for your vanishing, the
    hills
know nothing—I'll bury you deep in the scrub
so not even a dog will find you, and by evening
your old man—who's more white than black—will be
    searching gullies.

Young Bloke

And no matter what you've done to choke the gullies
they'd speak out in a language that'd just be noise
to you, but my dad and cousins would enter the evening
with the spirits behind them, and the morning
would be filled with a lament heard often through scrub
and it would wind like smoke and swallow the hills.

Farmer

No vanquished warrior nests on top of those hills
but one in complete command of his territory—the
    gullies
are fences but chasms for the uninitiated, the scrub
a place for collecting firewood and listening to the noise
of the trapped rabbit or poisoned fox, frozen stiff by a
    winter morning,
already rotting by a scarlet summer evening.

Young Bloke

You don't even know the names of evening
or the character of bones that give substance to the hills,
and the stories of even the brightest morning
are hidden from you, unna? And the gullies
carry away your soft 'initiations', that faint noise
of dissolving, like salt edging the scrub.

Farmer

It's all gibberish as far as I'm concerned, and as for the
    scrub,
I've plans for that—government reserves vanish by
    evening
when the torchlight, the bat sounds and nightjar noise
are quelled by rifle and chainsaw: they say out of these
    hills
aliens rise to abduct the lost traveller, that radiation's in
    the gullies,
that there's not a trace to be found of them by morning.

Young Bloke

You wadjelas have killed what you can see, and morning
is lonely because of it. You can't speak for me, and the
    scrub
hears my voice and sees me whatever you do. Most gullies
are made by your wrecking the scrub, but by evening

they hear the residue, and the laws of my mob surround
    the hills
and foil the tepid television-noise . . .

Farmer

You just think because you've had a few years of school
    that your noise
will change the way I see things: it'll be a bleak morning
when I change my tune, when my blisters will surrender
    these hills,
when I'll even see the tangled mess of bloody scrub
as having anything to do with you—if you're not out by
    evening
I'll come after you, and blood will run in the gullies.

Young Bloke

Hey, kuda, why don't you clean out your gullies?
Hey, kuda, why don't you plug up your noise?
Hey, kuda, why don't you see how the sun taints the
    evening?
Hey, kuda, why don't you dream through the morning?
Hey, kuda, why don't you stop wrecking the scrub?
Hey, kuda, why don't you have totems up in your hills?

Farmer

I cleared the tops of those hills, I have fenced off the gul-
    lies;
I hate not being able to see through the scrub, I am aware
    of every noise . . .

Young Bloke

He doesn't know us in the morning; he won't know us in
    the evening.

WANDOO SCORE

Wandoo tainted titanium white on a clear day
encased in blue, sharply lit and tempered cold,
frost ciphers, scores against shadows
folded away from the sun, wrenched
out of seasonal crevices, since the solstice;

up close, tracings of bark, spotted fade-away
and loud acclaims of knot and gnarl, black spider
webbing a crack or tear, gnats gripped by resin,
white ants hollowing a dead limb sticking out
like bone, lost from the looking up, those shadows

and atmospherics just allowing the shaky hand
to make its sign, through green oily film,
clumps of foliage overlaid and filling in where
rock-hollows and overhangs don't swallow light,
the Big Bang and its collapse built in,

warping windshift tempting rain gauge
on gently sloping lands down below, horses
   rampant in chemical
     green paddocks.

SURVEY

for Wilson Harris

Cleared paddocks are an impenetrable jungle
of introduced species; the surveyor scissor-steps
over Mediterranean Bugloss and Cape Tulip
and quips about storms. A kangaroo came up
the laneway last night and got tangled
in the fence—gazetted for a road
that we hope won't happen. The swampy
low-point that Mum's buying from a neighbour—
a sanctuary—is viewed from all angles.
Not much good for anything, he says,
noting herbicides would clear jungle
rapidly, expose soil as revelation.
In filing claims for shifting fencelines
his points of reference ignore orchids
and echidna scratchings, a reddish strip

of plastic scrapping with a southerly; a fetish,
it carries his spirit and our intentions,
to be replaced by wire when the deal
is done. In these layers there's no sifting,
for stripped-back the jungle would reveal
traces of poisoned arteries below, feeding
depressions, making sounds we're
      not trained to hear.

A DEFINING MOMENT

Trapped inside the cavity of my body
there is only and always twilight;
mallee scrub is like the hair that grows externally,
and through gravelly soil
something like blood runs.
                 Absolute faith
leaves a blank, though tension
stills cramps the heart and ties the gut in knots;
Jam tree is a hardwood
good for fence-posts and weapons; cut, it is sweetly
redolent.
       A player piano rolls, senses
replayed. After fire has ruptured
scrub and singed wandoo and powderbark,
winged wattle colonises again
into granitic soils, jam tree is there
as we are there: fire through cemeteries.
backing the soil to seal all as one grave,

deliverance coeval with soil density.
                                        Replete
with interaction, the dead
can almost afford to move around
but tend to stay, wars and incidents of violence
moving through them like pollen, crushing
red bonnets flowering almost profusely.
                                        My speech
is dribble from the snottygobble's foliage,
its anchor only in name or language
as a whole: a defining moment
like those who have something extracted by customs
and placed in quarantine,
                            this sickly sample,
tossed up in the driving waves of heat,
mercy pressed in sandy soil
by explorers who've
claimed precedent.

SAD COW POEMS

Affect flat as dung, or sludge
that slicks the gradient, the young
that drive an udder, as if a word
for 'cow' might make cattle
might make beef and might
make muscles
on seasons of less light—
late sunrise suppressing melatonin,

and that bell, sounding out,
as silver as a twisting acacia leaf
driven by a wild front coming in
to discharge the drought, the wanking machines,
gleam of the tanker
that'll feed the cream separator,
centrifuge making heavy
water.

Dairy farmers are fetishists.
They might arrange for sons
to beat you, or call their lawyers.
Either way, the truth is
they fondle genitalia.
As a best-case scenario
they suffer separation anxiety,
substituting mother's breasts.

Some don't eat them because they're large.
Geneticists will shrink them, even change
the colour of their flesh so they look
like chickens, with the colour and texture
of flesh remaining consistent.
The price will go up.
It will be a gourmet market
for refined sensibilities
and/or palates.

Molly B12 poked her head
through the door of the shack
most mornings. Her calf days
shortening. Some say pity
comes because of the size
of their eyes. Her eyes
were small, and their vocabulary
too immense for translation.

Intellectuals aspire
to cattle baronetcy.
They can control
in a way that they can't control
their peers. They can slaughter
in a way that they can't sexually
subdue. There's no getting away
from linking
sex and violence.

The old brown bull
said let's have anothery
down by the scrubbery
I'll supply the rubbery . . .

The old brown cow
said you can go to buggery
I'm not rootin' no more.

A city kid
in a city primary school
with familial connections

to the country
sang this to me
under the lantana tree.

Having lived on cow farms,
or inside cow farms—surrounded
by fences and cows and the apparently
conflicting sounds of slaughter
and the gum-booted, overalled
young men calling in, or maybe
I should say 'opening gates'
given the rush, udders so full
the milking shed is a relief—
for a grand total of eighteen months
or maybe two years, in the south-west
dairy and cattle areas,
I cannot speak cow still,
still, I cannot or never could
speak cow. Most of my time
spent with sheep,
I claim to understand
their words of pain
with some clarity,
whatever the dialect.

That serotonin rush, cow dung now pure
dust in drought, like snuff—the stuff
the oracle likes to inhale
before unsettling statesmen and warriors,
which might be one and the same; this big pastoral,
acrostic battle, imminent georgic

of the broken soil, shattered crust
that tread melaleuca and jam tree flats
and undulations, go down to the dam and creek
and Heidelberg lights
dappled and straited,
low to the horizon
and outbulked by the huge sky
with impressionable clouds
that can't rain, aren't painted in the right way
to let go their liquid as light
strikes sparks to fire the remaining
undergrowth on outcrops where hooves
gain little purchase, this breaking up.
In concordance, the Biblical imprimatur—
that seals the valves of every John Deere
or Case or even machine imported from Asia,
assuming it's been blessed
by Australian customs,
that glue that makes sinews
work hand in hand with bone,
while a tallow factory gets started
where they irrigate down south—
is listed from Isaiah, through Job, Leviticus,
Ezekiel, and Numbers, or the other way
round for the last two, with another Isaiah
in there, though Ezekiel's 'I have given thee
cow's dung for man's . . .' rings out
in the coprophilia of industry
and growth, and the fertilising
of paddocks stripped of all growth
in the opening-up of discourse.

My father was awarded a steer hide—red-brown
as the interior of Australia, quote unquote—
for a decade of service to the mining company.
There's nothing more to this anecdote.

The heat suffering is the suffering
of permanent winter, the sheets
of summer light and evisceration
the saturation of darkness
and veining of hillsides
after a cloudburst. All is darkness.
Light never stimulates the good vibes
of those chemicals that make *us* feel
all is okay when it isn't. It's the negative
that reverses inside and outside
the darkroom. Jersey cows
are particularly photogenic
and barely wince when the camera
automatically flashes
on a sunstruck summer's day.

Relishing the soft muzzle
and the warm moisture
around the nostrils, the light fur
that makes touch the central sense,
an organ in itself, about the mouth
that sub-electric intimation
that'll become arousal, stimulation
as you look to mate.

She milked the cow
after the earthquake
and surprisingly
it didn't hold back.
Stories of butter
in the bucket
have been the mainstay
of family myth
ever since.
The cow's name
was Princess.
It lived for another
couple of years,
though dried up
long before this.

The bull ring through his nipple
really was a bull ring,
and he demanded his girlfriends
use their panties
as a cape and spear him
with painted nails
as he rushed them.
He'd always admired
the get-up and pluck of matadors—
well-dressed and brutal,
with the backing of whole cities,
even countries.

City kid: What's a cow, Mum?

Mum: A large animal that lives in a field
and tastes a bit like McDonald's . . .

The stomach plug, flagrant to open
and check-up, ant colony the chamber,
the enzymal action, belly business,
fragrant, busy, the reaching in
and pulling out the mush, like the bin-composter
that turns around on its metal frame,
the sort that local industry can build and market,
you just throw in your grass clippings and the like,
make of it that extra stomach.

NIGHT MOMENT

Tail-lights—the going that's predatorial,
half-moon isolating cloudgaps, a code
that always adds an extra wheel, this fire-merge,
this deflection of having been an ever-changing
aerial landscape, most of which we've never seen.

MOWING

It's a rev thing this ingenu
contemplates as his bum vibrates
and ball-sack shakes, whipping
his sperm to a cream or frenzy,
or wiping out the last ones—
those missed by the herbicides
he dumps on the firebreaks.
It's hard to revel in winter greenery
chopped to a herby piquancy,
to feel a renewal come out of the red dirt
you know it disguises; strap-on, ride-on flirt,
he skirts fruit trees bare as the nudity
that takes him to the refrigerator
when the rest of the house sleeps,
his curvaceous paddocks close and smooth,
velvet on a flawed skin rising up
to meet him with every thrust.

CROP DUSTER JERK-OFF:
A POETRY OF ABUSE

The crop duster jerk-off is strafing just over the rise,
dropping clouds of fallout over 'green light' wheat;
he prides himself on his skill in tossing
the plane about: small, but *not* insect-like—
in spite of the warning-sign paint-job:
red and yellow stripes—it's a plane,
just a plane tanked up with chemicals.
He touts its fragility with an incessant buzz,
a throttling up that draws attention:
flicking about, if it comes down it will
take us all out. This isn't 'terrorism'?
There's a strong wind blowing in our direction.
The baby is not home today, for which I am grateful,
but it will come back to an invisible coating.
A new layer to our occupation. They kill to make us grow,
to feed the population. There's a chain
of profit as perpetual and cyclical
as a teething ring. Yelling into the tinctured air
makes you hoarse, and the pilot
gets off on it: it's in the loins, like reproduction,
through sperm count dropping
and the wheat changing colour.

THE SHITHEADS OF SPRAY

Under-ode, antediluvian reprisal,
seed vengeance, broad-leaf outrage,
seed-spray head kick, the pressure point
rumoured to have dropped Bruce Lee
in his tracks; haters of weeds,
haters of any more words
than needed: say it straight,
vandals, poofter-bashers, migrant-baiters,
dead gum lovers, parrot killers,
worshippers of spray-drenched fruit
that smiles without blight,
descendants of those who murdered
Yagan and chopped his head off,
sending it to Britain, Queen lovers
but haters of queens, lizard mockers,
snake beaters, makers of neat gardens.
There's no getting away from them.
Spray-drift sensurround, surround sounds
but furtively sibilant, odour-ploy.
Spray objectors have their cups of tea
laced with Antex while the shitheads of spray
graze sheep on dying grass
and smile benignly. Residuals denied,
the global plug: safe as table salt,
safe as houses, safe as oily rainbows
in winter light.

A SWARM OF PARAGLIDERS

Over the mountain they vacillate.
Not quite flies over dung—the mountain
is too good for that. And flies land—
these hover, and resist landing as long
as possible. They need the mountain
to stay up there—in their bullshit freedom,
coming down as far away from their launch place
as they can. Setting club records. Causing
distress to old men in fields and kids alone
in farmhouses when their cell phones
are out of range. I type looking up at them
over the mountain. Through camera lenses
they could see the detail of my scrunched face.
They are perverts, though consider
themselves without social boundaries
up there, above it all.
The drifts, lifts, drops, curves, and circlings
are sexual. They are frustrated. They are
of the same family as sky divers. When
I was in rehab almost a decade ago
one of the counsellors or nurses or doctors
or all of them suggested I go for a sky dive,
that its rush, its extremity, would satisfy
any craving that might be lurking
in the place where these things lurk.
I look up at these losers

and wonder if they've taken the bait: it's like that,
soul-fishing, killing the client, the victim:
up there, letting the air and a bird's-eye
view wash over their frustrations,
their brightly coloured chutes full of the sub,
high, luminous, caught up in the mix of control
and where the breeze might take you:
a thermal deceit.

RODEO

Ay-o-rodeo, hooray!
   Rodeo, rodeo, yay!
      Some say it will stay
      Even when they
Cart it far away, far away!

Wheel-less, it bogs down in clay,
   Leafy suspension dismay,
      Rust in the chassis
      Motor antsy,
The tray-top of the Rodeo

Is sieve-like, the Rodeo's
   tray-top is sieve-like. Hooray
      Ay-o-rodeo,
      Hey, rodeo!
A long way from the factory.

All about the enamelled
      Body, tufts of Cape Tulip
      Lash and flurry, strip
      Economy
Those robots in the factory.

O rodeo, Rodeo,
      Rodeo, rodeo, O,
         Under crow gestalt,
         Not far from salt,
We praise your brand-name, your shattered

Windows; the silver trimmings
      Stripped to the name Rodeo,
         Mauvaise foi, as your
         Aerial claws
The smoky air, rodeo!

Once we whipped you up into
      A lather, a glint in your
         High beam, those burn-outs
         We used to tout
At crossroads, Rodeo, a show!

Ay-o-rodeo, hooray!
      Rodeo, rodeo, yay!
         Some say it will stay
         Even when they
Cart it far away, far away!

VIGILANTE ECLOGUE

Vigilantes

He was at our women's windows
when we were at the pub or working late,
they'd hear him snuffling about.
The morning would always reveal
something upset or not quite right:
the lines on the rotary hoist snapped,
an upturned flower garden.
No way you'd leave underwear
out overnight: it'd be soiled
or slashed by sunrise. Messages
in blood or shit or mud
would grace the walls of church
or town hall, and once he even
profaned the pub. He spread malicious gossip,
said Ben's wife had slept with Joe,
and Joe's wife with her own sister.
He said our minister liked young girls,
and that the local cop sold drugs.
So you've gotta understand,
we had to punish him: crack
his skull open and pour some sense in.

Victim

They well nigh killed me, slaughtered
me like they do their sheep and pigs,
hogtied and threatened to sodomise me
like they 'do their bitches'. Every word
they say I said, I deny . . . though I know
why they'd think it's me because I know
a thing or two that goes on behind the scenes
in this town. They hate me because I keep cats,
and throw rocks at their dogs when they piss
on my car wheels. They gutted one of my Persians,
and called me a wog bastard. They turned
my house to ash and after three months
in hospital I came out to nothing.
Now it's me who's got to move—
everyone in town's behind them,
saying 'they're ours, born and bred'!
They both played on the footy team
and married farmers' daughters.
I know a thing or two that goes on
behind the scenes in this town.

Vigilantes

The town cop would have fixed him
if he'd found the perfect moment;
just too much heat to let him have
his way. The town almost boiling over
and public meetings and shoutings-down

in the street. If a bloke can't protect
his missus, stand up for the bit
of land that's his, then what's
the world coming to? We've got to back
our prime minister in his war against
the freeloaders and terrorists
who'd fill our country with their prejudices!
We've got to stand up to them!
Just listen to that bludger's name, if you can
pronounce it. We trust him as much
as we'd trust a black fella.

Victim

One of those ladies said to me:
'you're no better than a black fella . . .';
then made a joke about my donga.
Classy, very classy. This town
that raves between hot and cold: it gets
so crisp on mid-winter mornings
that it jolts memories out of childhood.
I can barely piece it together. The
'back then . . .' As a child there was dust
and I watched with just enough
understanding as a neighbour
cried secretly when his mother died.
What's wrong with that? He never knew.
I said nothing. I did him small favours
to absolve the guilt, and because
he needed it. My own mother
was somewhere nearby. There were crows

in that place too. Majestic birds,
they're not scared of my cats.
Those blokes shoot all the parrots,
run them down in cars:
and yet they rang the conservation people
and told them my cats were killing off
the native wildlife.

Vigilantes

He just doesn't belong. Never
made an effort, muttering his mumbo jumbo
at odd hours of the day, hung up
on staring out past the town hall,
as if someplace else were a magnet. Wishful thinking—
not one of us meeting in that haloed hall
wanted him near us; he never belonged.
His mangy cats killed the parrots,
and he smelled of perfume
and toilets. We've no doubt he's a poofter.
He rarely went to the city,
but we're sure it was buggery
that drew him towards
the lights and shadows.
He planted bloody morning glory—
a forbidden plant—a weed—
and it spread all over
the goddamn town!

Victim

I get lonely. Sometimes I step out and listen.
I've always done that. I've never hurt anyone,
and it's nothing to do with religion.
In some ways, I believe as my neighbours
believe, differently. They suspect me
because I speak out rarely in public.
Here on the edge of paddocks I feel safe,
despite my head gaping open, and poison
being poured into my wounds. The cats
were already here—abandoned
by the townsfolk. I didn't bring them.
They came to my back door, sick and scared.
I fed them, so they would eat less parrots.
All people are welcome at my house—
were welcome at my house—
if they could manage to ignore my ways,
and shift through the here and now
which has a past that's ash,
a future that can't take root.

ACT 4

REFLECTORS: DRIVE 4

for Tracy

Leaving this morning
you would have been blinded
driving into the sun, driving
by guesswork, until skirting
boundaries and rejecting
interference; it's a choice
to drive away from heat, to avoid
the catastrophe of burnt sight;
sun in the mirror, it drives you,
its threats posthumous, edited
out. So I time this with your return,
at so many metres and so many words
per minute, per hour. Tracking
you with text, and your being conscious
of it: a kind of lure, a magnet maybe,
wishful thinking and ambiguity
as the risks and need for concentration
foil any gameplay. Heavy traffic
up Greenmount Hill, past the Red Witch's
house, birthplace of your daughter,
and mine after eight of her ten years,
to the point of worrying about: it's
of us, part of we is missing, they are me.
Verbal play. And with her rages,

her episodes, her sudden switches,
we grow closer: trinity or triptych,
on display to see how we'll hold up:
we will. The white-tailed black cockatoos
might be flying across State forests,
jousting signs and fences, rapid over jarrah.
It's not divination—if it's true at all—
I just know showers are on the way,
and despite this high contrast, starkly
clear day, the best driving conditions
are concentrations and an awareness
that something might happen—and this
can come just as readily at night,
in heavy rain. Expect the worst. Drive
'defensively', but don't fight the traffic.
The speed camera will be at Mundaring,
a fait accompli, and drivers will drive
tens ks below the highest speed limit
and forty ks over the lowest, maintaining
the same pace as if in a dream. Consistent?
A literature of driving, a reconstituting the flesh
of a kangaroo so impacted by a prime mover
that irony kicks in to dissemble carnage.
It's what you do to keep driving. And
watch Sawyer's Valley, cop-land as well,
and place of bush meets the outer
consciousness of the city, trouble
never far below the surface. You could
joke: witness, the shooting club,
car rallies, a tavern doing a brisk
lunchtime trade. But that's all projection.
The run between the Valley and The Lakes

modulates—traffic keen to break out
on the Great Eastern Highway, swinging
north and east, disconsolate beneath
flightpaths into Perth Airport,
down over the Scarp, down the hill
into the city. Our daughter said:
from up here even the city
is exquisite. As if it were part
of nature. They're clearing more bush blocks
and an inversion layer forms
even in winter. And cold nights
bring wood-haze: outside the shed
the arc welder is spitting, fusing metal
and air and flux. Its light bends
and warps, an increment of the sun
now behind you, cutting up rear vision
and blinding oncoming traffic.
Each car and truck you pass
negotiates with your presence.
Communion, correspondence, negotiation.
The indeterminate features. Only
part of the body visible at the best
of times, deciphered through colour
and shape, model, registration number
if you're quick enough. Unless obscured
by the sun's intensity. There's a truckbay
not long before The Lakes—on your right
heading home—across passing lanes,
double white lines. It commemorates
a name—I've often wanted to stop
to read the sign. Was he a trucker
who lost his life? A citizen of the district?

We'll read that sign together sometime.
It's good to fill in the spaces on the map
or to leave the map alone. I checked
the fuel yesterday—you'll be fuelling
at The Lakes, the halfway point.
You might pick up a newspaper
if they've any left this late in the day—
you walk right past them when you go to pay.
Like me, you feel free breaking away
onto the York Road. Though it's a false
freedom, a placebo. Down in the city,
your daughter, trying to understand
her problem, waiting to turn off
at The Lakes and say, We're on our way
home. As you've inherited or absorbed
or taken on my lifetime's memories,
so has she. We're all as connected
to this place, and all as uncomfortable
about how close we feel. The traditional
custodians are heard, cars drive on,
sheep and cattle trucks take bends
beyond stability, living loads
crushed, internal injuries ignored.
Language is never incidental, or coincidental.
Heartstrings in Yorkshire connect with limbs
in the wheatbelt of Western Australia.
And you'll pass Serena Park where my brother,
your brother-in-law, is shearing. You won't know
if he's had a good day, and I don't know
if you'll sense it. The ideologies
mix with the tarmac, might spark
reflectors, though it's probably

the sun again, getting lower,
but still active. Bitumen absorbs
reason and fragmented light
as you pass pasture on one side
of the road and wandoo on the other.
Light can't be categorised here,
and surfaces and interiors rupture
like high gloss on gravel or blue-metal.
It barely makes sense as art, and can be
dangerous. The arc welder cracks
in the background—it is sound,
barely visual. It upsets the flow
of electricity, and the grinding power
vibrates in its fury. Driving together,
there are points that mark progress.
Pinker trees on high ground,
sweeping curves, snaking bends,
Mount Observation turnoff, St Ronan's Well . . .
there are the creeks—13 and 6-mile,
the property we thought of buying,
rehabilitating on the edge of Wambyn Reserve.
Monetarism and ownership collate place
like tyre reflectors and it wanders away,
the road never that decisive. Listening
to music, working over emotions, gathering
facts—the different markers of conversation.
Or marked against a slow car that you can't pass,
or a particularly long truck that offers
no hope of escape. The heater not working,
cold forcing a hand under a leg,
one hand on the wheel. Sheep on a ridge.
Variegated colours of soil exposed

with drought. Scarrings of frost.
Dull pull of the moon waning
to nothingness. It becomes
an occupation of time and space:
the effects of concentration,
deployment of relevant skills.
And soon, maybe now, maybe
simultaneous to the production
of these words, through Cut Hill,
bisected by Cut Hill Road. The land
there is for sale as well—one of us
noticed the other day. It changes hands
politely. Some renege on payments,
go bankrupt. Others change titles
and make a packet. The tracks
of others are trampled and gouged out.
Rock-piles gathering at practical
intervals platonic in their rearrangement
of the structure. For Sale signs
hide nothing, dissemble nothing.
And then, just past the five kilometre
sign, Morris Edwards Drive. Who was Morris
Edwards? How did the naming happen?
The back road home. The mountain
in sight. Again, the colours!
Ulster Road, Bland Road, the crossroad.
And into the mountain. I will hesitate. Stop.
I will walk out and see if you're arriving,
you're that close now. What's this
got to do with words? It's time, mathematics.
It's chemical, reactive. Three or four minutes
and I pick up on this text again. I listened

hard, watched. The outcrop of Mount Brown
seemed sharp and indifferent, light in York gums
like a morose bushfire, the thin green pasture
a false promise, nothing. The sun
is stronger than I imagined in here,
inside the shed, typing; my timing
out—slightly out—I know
that you are near.

MAP: LAND SUBJECTED TO INUNDATION

So that's salt, *the* salt, wonderland wanderlust
comeuppance, coo-ee refractor, TV static-inducer,
sullen receptor when crystals dampen
and melt, form a suggestion, this land
on the York map, Avon District, South-west Land
    Division,
South-west Mineral Field, fed by stream intermittent,
as high winds are ossified into not-that-far-off
contours and cliffs, trigonometrical station
                        on the infinitesimally
small reserve crowning Needling Hills, which the now—
    'owners'
won't let us climb:
              so how does that feel?
                      Uncle Jack's
old homestead 'Avonside' is listed, a square peg in a round
    hole
transmuted by grid convergence against the sheet centre,

                                        interferon
fighting intrusion of recollection,
                              that road we cut-up
on the Kwaka 100, small cc'd trail-bike that was big to us
and raced twenty-eight parrots in their lifts and dips
drawn out:
            they really *do* drag you off.
                                    Contour lines
show a gradual falling away—not that dramatic.
                                      Wallaby Hills
at 59.2300 ha is only a semi-reasonable patch
set aside
            for the conservation of flora and fauna,
                                    and we know
the fence is down on the Melbong Creek side and sheep
wander through into a place where their dead brethren are
    dumped,
grazing diminishing species of plants.
                                  This isn't for the sake
of the sheep, but the farmer extending the realm of grazing
to bulk them out, add a dimension to the quality of wool.
The landloss, water-tones sourced in the telephone paddock,
house dam paddock, running down through salt
as a drawcard, like an osmotic filter, sheep skin
a catalyst to seepage, and salt clustering
all about—
            it's the shape,
                        the string in solution,
wide-eyed and close to formations,
                                  avatars and hucksters,
deeply serious holders of the 'Bolya',
                                  whom you respect
and fear:

in subjugating and making his *Vocabulary*
of the Dialects of South Western Australia, Captain Grey
noted of the Boyla-ya-gaduk, that flight and dispersal
in air are a pleasure, had at will, or a pleasure to transport
in such a fashion, as invisible they'll force entry as a shat-
    tering
of quartz and consume flesh,
                            these chips of white and apricot quartz
littering the waste of the place now labelled as 'land
                                                subjected
to inundation', that we call The Salt.
                            This creek or system of creeks
came out of the homeplace, fed by any poisons applied
to enhance the crops, fuel the generator that pushed out
little over thirty volts,
                    creek system that fed and feeds Pitt Brook
that feeds the Mackie River that feeds the Avon, con-
    tributing
to the salinity of the valley, this salt mine, this source
vicariously 'ours',
                    left behind, enriching
the nation's coffers, comeuppance, a sullen receptor
where crystals dampen and melt.

YORK-SPENCER'S BROOK ROAD

I have a pavilion of land-folds in my vision, no
inland sea, just roadside drainage, scorched river, cored-
    mountain range
evoking leeward hills;

                    my works and days pass through bales
and sheep, drenched and collected burrs from summer's
    end stubble,
overtly aware of the remaining trees, ludicrous lack of
    shade,
their urge for seedlings.
                        Railroad, creek, farm gate, crossing
telegraph stripped off wire and intentionality: our
    daughter's
school bus does the long drive through burning off,
the intentional fire season has started, the windrows
can be seen in their combustion: extinguishment
a cabalistic dialogue I remember from somewhere else.
                                                    This
the valley, river running irregularly alongside the road,
a fraction of its deep-hold self, running level and dry,
a treeline of flooded gums, York gums, jam tree,
roadside foliage as well. There are points where a polygraph
would detect a change, or take it as standard
to tell truths and lies of quartz against: flood points,
crests, the road so narrow cars almost touch
in passing.
                    You see people walking or standing
even here: at ploughing or seeding or harvest times,
and sometimes between gate-posts of a tree-lined
drive, the trees not of these parts.
                                            Stone rooms
and car bodies, a gravel pit embracing a pyre of dead-grey
York gum trunks, branches. In time, they'll be burnt,
because they're in the way, or unproductive, or irritating
to the eye. The gravel has the taint of salt, white crystals
undoing laterite and clay, easing out of the run-off cut
    marks.

So, memory is sectioned out of the aerial photo,
and heavy haulage fragments the road edges. In this,
a theory of disaster, in the farmhouse centred in wasted
fields, the panopticon. Closely, a black-shouldered kite
hooks a mouse, and an unrecorded species of possum
feeds nightly on Crown land, thin about the railway line.
Here, dragonflies don't need water? I roam here,
along the edges, flattening against the blue-metalled
rail bank against the cars, all cars. Sky-divers
lumber, stall, drop. All I want is truth and to evade
the herbicide residues. Keeping it down, keeping it open.
Wodjil—poverty bush—skirts somewhere, maybe further
     north,
or east where the last salmon gums—the first salmon
     gums—
appear just outside the town, their level tops dry clouds,
electrically green. Storms come from these places,
prime on this strip of road, submerged in storm,
shooting gallery. Brazen, lightning welds the edges,
those bloody shoulders, hazard lights picked up
as alien: the telephone down in houses,
the prisoners out: fox dead on the road
heading to Northam, place of the supermarket, and more.

QUELLINGTON ROAD

for Tim Cribb

The back way to Meckering cuts fault-line,
earth-rip, roads never thin as they look:
                                    avarice
has bite where the needle of asphalt runs through rises,
falls, tamed breakaways. To take a run past
salt clefts, paddocks to be burnt, less bushland
than there might be: the roads lassoing
at points where the glare might take you
and the family over the line to block the sun
in a window, the disc plough semi-abandoned
in the right angle of fenceline, these architectures
of a violent sublime where the awe is worn down,
high points low, though returning into the tableau
Bakewell radiates, its towers cabalistic: I believe
shadows cast by wedge-tailed eagles are absorbable
rarities.
            Where else am I to home in on?
                                    The travel bug
a dung-eater, a godless transportation where culture
is the memory of a road-side stop, York gums
barely holding out against salt, a tower silo
gutted by fire and neglect;
                            these excursions we make,
these sightings we keep largely to ourselves;

Duck Pool Road,
a reserve of sorts, an almost dry Mortlock, what's there,
brackish, laden with algae. The birds small—flicking
insect life; overall, a marker, the *heard* in the niche,
the disrespected, the quelled.
I still cannot understand
why someone shot our neighbour's horse and dumped it in
the dam,
nor why someone shot close to the house. Vestigially, I think
this when the paddocks are bare, when the windrows snake
three dimensionally through the road, and science-fiction
is laid bare as having little to say—
it's all here,
where people are few, where road-sign distances are aber-
rations,
where the survey point warns you off and salt forms in
road-ruts.
These are the best prayers for human effort I can manage,
these desiccated lines to the road, to the deceptive
light that surrounds—
so bright the shadows are burnt out,
silhouettes wells struck where water won't flow,
plant machinery touching off no memories.

MOKINE ROAD

The rage is not the damage
but threats and twisting, skating
across a top-dressed road: bunkered

within fields of central heating,
even sunlight an image of warmth
worthless, stir-crazy gleaning
of photographs, this presence
built out of nothing;
                              bruising cross-season
a restraint of infectious yellow, fringed
by chemical green, scales of cockatiels
hazing as the semi-arid zone bumps south,
those deflective fields of native grass trees
promptly grazed by sheep;
                              the lacerations
and growths of rock, chips off the old block,
decorative syntax nosed by echidnas,
eyelets of rust from star pickets and gnarls
in wandoo,
                              the clearing done by males with drinking
problems or chemical imbalances, their daughters
resentful or fighting the voices: the fading green
of their eyes is concurrent with desiccation,
dehydration, removal of water—after schooling,
some travel to the city and join the CSIRO,
returning to track rare diseases in parrots
their brothers shoot by the score;
                              pink pokers
biting the skin, ash of firing, scars
they can't see and they don't get the irony
despite an addiction to horror films.
                              At harvest,
machinery to slash and cull ruts the road,
a short cut to Toodyay, convolution
of vistas and difficult family histories.

Shade
in this quarter season means something slightly
different. The sun almost an anti-psychotic.

BORROW PIT

for Andrew Duncan

To gnash the gravel, 'winning' they call it,
a pit just in from Mokine Road, down Waterfall—the roads
hereabouts, the gravel tops that slide like watersheds,
top-dressed with laterite efficacy, as where the bush is
   demolished,
twenty feet deep the clay and gravel are extracted,
now a dumping pit—household, property-making waste,
piles of dead trees and dead sheep, runnels
and washouts, this God in lines; at the rim
powderbarks, mallee, a centrifugal gulley,
parrot bush . . .
          bulldozed sub-edges,
                  radar dish, deflecting
messages back to the source—this being no place
for thermometers;
        so winning your winning ways,
so borrowed and charcoal of visited fires,
shadows that contradict a fireban, small birds
in cutting bushes,
            the twenty-eights almost discrete;
                  it imposes itself,

this discovery, more so for climbing up into the mallee,
more so for a stay shorter than we like;
                                        what can be sourced
where a lingering wildlife owe it all to the roads
insisted, good state of repair, rarely used
and only by a few farmers and their families,
commodity,
                the 'ute shooting thing', power trap,
horrified, those shadows. I position myself,
this gravel pit, the bark stripping
from flooded gums a few miles away
where on *warning* land the gravel falls,
runs thinly when dry is dead-set everywhere. Ennui
is this God I know though can't feel: willing
on pitted stone, looking molten
in bush about the pit, like meteorites
coagulated, decked out like a living museum—speccy.
The body clock is a barometer, like the veins that knit
with our partners sleeping together, or alone, bind us to
    the bed,
stimuli from the dead.
                            The stark blue sky sucks primaries
from the pit—winning gravel. Its cadenza
shape gives the illusion of water or epithets.
It takes scree to collude where water
is past or a ruse—I search them out, these places
to fill in the space—an emptiness that clarifies
pluralities. They are like letters or signs of grammar—
even syntax in its entirety—scooped out. The sounds of
    parrots
and honey-eaters an antidote to language,
                                        an antidote

to borrowed visions. Shit, what of me? So far below
the thin surface, fertility . . . reseeding will bring trees
flourishing out of the gravel clay. They plant them, some-
    times,
to fill in the gap. A reclamation that might
lead to reserve status, a nominal forbidding
that will still attract triple twos, kids-on-weekends with
    twenty-twos,
cracking hornet hollow points,
                        the chest-fuck twelve gauge:
they might even claim environmental
good husbandry, ridding the vicinity, the borrow pit,
of rabbits and foxes . . . and we know what too many roos
can do. Wankers.
                In cast-offs we meditate, the midday glow
down through the branches of a powderbark chewing the
    gulley,
chemical in its winning way,
                        the unnameable odour
of its bark, the nameable odour of its leaves.
In this heat, it's not hard to taste a place
from a few days ago, a year ago, from childhood.
In middle lives the shadows dilute in paddocks,
cleared spaces, and gravel pits the tear-away places
ripped up by teenagers on Kwaka trailbikes:
                            how much
of this penance acquires its vantage point, its skulduggery
of prayers, its wrestling with fence-post pivots, the plough
disks, the antipathy of trucks bogged to the axles
in sweat.
        I borrow those moments, those high notes
of anticipation the early morning galahs ripping about,

chucking fits by the low ground;
                              I borrow words
from before I could speak, the tones of wandoo and mallee,
intricacies of roots, and palettes of gravel
that stare us in the face, trunks horizontal, parallel
to the rippling undersurface, those winning ways.

REDNECK REFUTATION

I didn't connect regardless
how much I participated, it's a vocab thing
though not to do with skills of expression;
                              ejecting bullets
from the breech, freezing whole carcasses
of home-slaughtered sheep, the contradictions
roll the same roads, and families
still come to visit:
                    crops in the bush, sullen days
coming down off bad speed, scoring from the old bloke
shacked up with teenage girls,
                              his bull terrier
crunching chickens;
                    a flat in the city is a deal
that can go either way, and the economics
of the paddock are the call-girl's profit;
                                   the Ford Fairmont
runs against the speed camera, and blind grass
poisons sheep—sightless like the minister
among his flock,

                    the school teacher,
                              the father
who won't let his son play netball because it will turn him,
like an innocent bitten by a vampire, into a pervert—or
    worse—
a poofter. Outside, you can't know that those
who speak in short, inverted sentences
always have fences in a state of disrepair,
                              line length
and wire length are directly proportional,
eloquent subdivider of land, intensive pig farmer,
will let nothing in or out, though the space around the
    pig-shed
is large and open, mainly used for hay cutting
while all sons play Guns N' Roses' *Appetite for Destruction*,
timeless classic . . . apotheosis, serrated road edge
where a termite mound astoundingly remains intact: there
are no generics, no models of behaviour.
                              It's not that my
name is a misnomer: it's who owns
a particular conversation.

HOME

1. Malapropisms, Homophones, and Synonyms

Back in Cambridge
you'll recall
being up near

the jarrah canopy,
rough bark aerial towers,
the granite tors
lichen-covered, scriptic
and scintillate with internal light
despite the pumped-up clouds
swaggering in a low sky;
rock-split and valley-cut
reminiscent—the names
have slipped from short-term
memory, or data paths
have altered, or codes
from lacklustre translators
have confused the picture:
in-micro the residue
of fruiting bodies
might be stupas
from a passage
read earlier, glass fragments
brightening leaf-litter
and kangaroo droppings,
a mixture of clover that's blown in
and creeping mosses,
riptops from drink cans,
mosquito legs high tensile
bacilli rods—not sculpted—
a bird-call that's interspersed
with tinnitus—Grantchester
thrushes—native grasses
and sour weed, torn parabola
of tinfoil, its dull reflective
scatter bulbs tapping ink

and the flow of Gooralong Brook
in its groove, a surface
within a surface, neither stable,
flow of data between magnetic bankheads,
hardwired with jarrah roots,
corruptible like dieback and chemicals,
the drop of exhaust as four-wheel
drives trot along with trout anglers
and 'bogs' race past dog walkers
who drive station wagons
and utes with cages on back;
corruptible like processing
black cockatoos, early monoplanes,
berserk stands of bamboo in the brook
and termite traps
shrouded in black plastic
topping caked-over tree stumps:
that's colony that's registration
that's a declaration of wattle
about the barbecues
and tables.

2. 'Killed by the Fall of a Tree . . .'

A bright day. The wind gusts
In fits and starts, white cockatoos
Saunter past, their choked cries
Almost leisurely . . . marking time.
Glancing up into the tangled canopy,
Light caught by gravity,
He opens his mouth, as if to say:

I've walked this way year in, year out,
A track worn to a cliché, the front
History, but this the forecast:
How silently we foresee,
'Killed by the fall of a tree.'

3. Feeders

Streamed elites generate insults;
Dead set slime emergent
On pipes tucked beneath the road, compassed
At crossings: who was Cold Harbour? Where?
Stark white trees—sapless—
Spread out, washed-up pre-fossils
Farmed by microbes,
Gould League twitched nest-robbers
But they're only kids;
Rainfall data zones
As verb, the pathology of sticky ground:
It's performance.

Car bodies and the drums
Of whirlpool washing machines
Implode: a dozen ways of storing waters,
Creeks that go nowhere in childhood
Kick-start wattle trees,
Sub-surface, rock skip,
Asbestos houses too close to the main road
Which whips past loudly,
Until it falls to gravel
Adrift   interference

Or water out of a hill
Below points of maximum
Absorption:
A gnamma theory
That can't be ignored
And this is science
As much as metaphor:
Can truth be appropriation?
Para-rhyme whittled away

To pick up, to tie it together,
To say it begins or ends here:
Past tense, second person.

4. At the Base of the Hill

Broken surface yields red soil:
Celtic hair roots webbing folds
and premonition of terraces,
new buildings, parodies
of secret societies.
Those names we don't know
how to pronounce, shade-cragged
air, and balloons of paddy melons
poisoning edges.
As the front blasts through,
the deeply cored hill
spikes and strikes upwards,
winter-bright, and all it supports—
memory, tallow-barked trees,
conflicting histories choked

by rungs of just-emerging crops:
plough lines like arguments
in other people's houses.
The light stops.
Blank night works vapours.
It all hangs about, weeps,
redresses the picture.

5. High Point

A single strand of barbed wire
Twists through the picture,
The palette a spreading
Aerial fracture, dividing
Tracks and taut speech
Along the thorny border.

I'm here, at the high point,
Not recognising my own
Terms of reference—
Date of birth, visible scars.

New connections are made:
Mains power and scheme water,
Fresh telephone lines,
But the mail won't come out here.

Snowy—the black Labrador
From next door, brings to mind
Ray, the biker and JP
Who died on his Harley

A few weeks ago. Charcoal
And ash from the burn-off
Uneasy over the ground.
His absence is everywhere.

The single strand of barbed wire
Linking cross-eyed star pickets,
Dividing properties—his family
Over there, doing what you do

When love is stripped bare. I never
Met him though his portrait
Is built out of conversation.
Larger than life, I'm told.

The rains have come
Heavy and all at once.
Compacted time delayed
And unleashed. A retainer wall

Stops the house pad washing away.
It looked like drought when Ray
Was still around, but there's
Enough rain now to touch
A denuded water table's highpoint,
Washing ash into the graves.

6. Oral Languages

Burnt letters of an oral language,
Sign   shape   scansion: crisp leaves

Flouncing over time-rings, coup de grâce
Scripting charred trunks, that summer
Flaming, rushing through tinder-dry grass,
Rustling sparks within sparks:
Back then, that other season.

Dual-wheeled tractors pierce clay,
Seedstock unstable, unlabelled,
Filling cereal boxes with numbers
And subtexts. Suburban overlay—
It's soil and rock beneath the freeways,
Micro-organisms of another language,
Ownership and overlay
Are not solely about rural spaces.

A creek connects properties:
A laneway that might be called up,
Might be drained and raised.
But now it's run-off—feeding
House dams, roadside drains.
The gravel darkens. The town Council
Sends workers out to check the flow.

Ownership. Slippery when wet.
Metal signs reflect the muddy,
Tongue-tied ground. Sun glares
Down on a cut in the hill—solid rock
Elegiac, a focal point for rainbows
Intersecting: looking up, caught
In open air, cushioned by the magnet
Until the field tilts and words fill papers.

FATIGUES

It's astonishing how connections
are suppressed as the square men in peaked hats
and fatigues let the body—the carcass—of a stag
drop over the tailgate of a four-by-four pick-up,
no sissy SUV, but a monster like an F250, gloating like the
   strip
of glittering advertising that runs across the base
of the cable TV broadcast, self-advertising, smug
parody of itself;
                    two Amish men—twins it would seem—
no more than late teens or early twenties, shopping
for glow-flighted arrows and pretzels from Wal-Mart,
their buggy parked in a distant corner
                                        of the car park,
as if they don't mind walking out past the cars,
                                        the horse
shitting behind its blinkers.
                              Looking for another entry point
to the Kokosing Trail, we happen on Danville. Katherine
mis-remembers it as the anchor-point of a school bike
   excursion.
A pick-up in the car park celebrates bow hunting—
                                        a luminous
sticker. The town reminds us of somewhere in the south-
   west
of Australia, say Bridgetown where I lived for a year

and was run out with my friends because we were
'hippy shits' and 'dyke-fleas', where our water

                                        was poisoned
and a town roo shooter watched from highground,

                                        binoculars
glinting in the setting sun, incarcerated in brittle
cold air—

                yes, I keep bringing this up, but it can't
be written out in a few metrically neat stanzas,

                                        especially
in a beat that neither the shooter nor his intended victims
would recognise. Incidentally, bunches or clusters
of men leave from the city for such expeditions,
so it's not just of the country, though most see
it as a country thing.

                        In Washington DC and northern
Virginia a sniper is game-playing—Fox Media, core
of an evil empire, describes death as 'picking them off',
and talks in terms of 'headshots'. They interview
hunters on shooting ranges, the season opening. The NRA
doesn't want the signatures of gun-barrels to be written
into a DNA record;

                        I have been around roo shooters
and cat killers and have myself killed birds and foxes and
    rabbits
and fish and insects;

                        I have also killed a ram
with a broken neck. That's well over twenty years ago: I say
this so you know that I know what I'm talking about.

                                        Images
are scarce or toxic,

                blurred by the changing season.

                                        Blood

mingles with altering leaf-colour,
                              red fall-through,
glowing in the fallout of open fires,
                              illuminating
the village taxidermist's. The art of these lines
is to show no animal feeling. My blood might be
tainted, but I'm probably not human. Maybe it's language
that traps me,
                'hunter'/poet, sacerdotal flasher:
                                        understand
that these killers might see miracles too, and experience
God's love, and have their prayers listened to.
                                        But what they
offer in return—God so reliant on goodwill—is confused,
is an hallucination weighed down with the addictive
taste of plasma and red corpuscles,
                              anointed communities
focussed through crosshairs at turkey shoots and fox hunts
and rabbit kills, cultural preservatives that kill them slowly,
anecdotal as inheritance, familial polyps
sticking out like bad beacons,
kids feeling the rush differently
and obviously wanting more.
                              When the light's
not quite right in the scope
a faun can become a witch, a bad spirit;
                              alcohol
is not essential—fizzy drinks full of sugar
do a similar thing,
                these trees and hands
marked by powder burns,
                        paying homage
to the dead they never knew.

THE DAMAGE DONE

Someone is revving the shit out of a chainsaw;
We look up from flatlands to the wooded summit,
Up past the hillside paddocks, up at the place of law.

Policemen don't go there, it's not their law,
Whitegums cast no shade over sheep, roots of wattle
    vibrate,
Someone is revving the shit out of a chainsaw.

After the heatwave, vandals cut wood like straw,
The damage done out of sight, we hear them harvest into
    night,
Up past the hillside paddocks, up at the place of law.

Tomorrow, in extrovert morning light, it will be hard to
    ignore
Their lines of light, ghosts of the outcrop trapped in
    granite,
Someone is revving the shit out of a chainsaw.

Night birds stuck in raw, dark air, left to claw
Phantoms and microwaves, asides in the script,
Up past the hillside paddocks, up at the place of law.

Down here, the parrots have returned—there are more
Than we thought. They scan for seed out of habit.
Someone is revving the shit out of a chainsaw,
Up past the hillside paddocks, up at the place of law.

'ONCE A FARM BOY,
ALWAYS A FARM BOY':
A GLOBAL POSITIONING ECLOGUE

(Knox County, Ohio, USA; Avon Valley,
Western Australia)

Knox County

Corn and Angus bulls, chickens and black-faced sheep,
now streams of genetically bolstered soy beans,
a day-time job sparking people's powerpoints—IT
connections, though no interest myself: did all that
during the Gulf War, and before. Never got to know
those people, though I know my buddies and their families
as well as you can know anybody, on the weekends
when the kids are plugged into PlayStation—rated
TEEN—I throw the quad around, pop a clip
and mow down targets. Not much under crop,
not like when I was a kid: got it all in before
Halloween; it will be a good Thanksgiving—
it's warm for this time of year. The snows
will probably be deep, and the roads icy.

Avon Valley

It's been a life of wandering, waiting for the farm
to be broken up. I want my heritage in land,
my brothers and sisters will go for the money—

growing families and all that. I'm single,
though have bunked down with a few women
over the years—a few townies, some rousties
from the sheds: the women who work there
are as rough as guts, into physical sex,
if you get my meaning. They usually
turn up at the pub with their car
and an old man somewhere trying to track
them down. I've had a bikie search
me out at the shed with a self-loading rifle—
I got him pissed and he turned his anger
against the cops. Doing six years.

Knox County

Despite the guns, we don't fight.
I've never hurt my wife. I'd shoot
anyone that did. We're part of a community,
and have enough food and ammo bunkered
to hold off for twelve months at least.
I tell you, it's God's own country here—
the moon-stained walnut tree
arching over the house, no need
for curtains or fences. Our neighbours
know who we are. We know ourselves.
They can listen through windows
with lasers, *they* know where you are.
We know of the parents of our parents,
the home countries that made us,

that we freed ourselves from. In God
we trust, but don't trust foreigners.
In Danville they let the children off school
to enjoy the first day of hunting season
with their families; on another day
they cook and eat raccoons.

Avon Valley

I will take back what is mine.
I know the ways of those that came before.
I will wire the paddocks and reclaim the salt land.
I will get a decent wife—private school,
settler stock—to share my bounty,
provide me with children. I will drink
beer without guilt, and innovate
at harvest time. I will know the markets.
I will bend to no government.
I will hunt vermin. I will kill off
diseased stocks and improve the wool-clip—
the South Africans have been after
merino sperm for years.
It's God's own country here—
the moon-stained wandoo tree
arching over the house.
We impale foxes, cook up
rabbits that haven't been done over
by myxomatosis.

Knox County and Avon Valley

The air tastes different. Rumours
proliferate like oil prices. The government
has a responsibility to ease our discomfort.
We are the heartland, the core
of the new world. We read papers now.
Shit in, shit out. We project
our God, our country, the moon-stained
trees overhanging our houses;
we sense the same moon cutting trails
and furrows over the fields, the paddocks,
impelling, lying in wait:
the sun red, bloodied by our resistance,
our mutual aid.

⪘⪘⪘ THE ⪘⪘⪘
LAST ACT
(5)

REFLECTORS: DRIVE 5

Part I

> *'Admittedly I err by undertaking*
> *This in its present form . . .'*
> —JAMES MERRILL

Sufficient time has passed to prompt
a test of memory. Sufficient time
to travel the road where weathers
and times of day are folded or blended
into one. Who drives? You and I or a family
member on the way to work or an appointment
in the city—notice how hard it is to focus
the journey towards luminescence,
always turning headlights back
towards an inner light. What properties
prefer an ownership, prefer a settlement
of coordinates and value? Back on the market,
the old place still has those horseshoes
turned upside down, embossed, water-marked
with luck running out, woven
through interlock mesh, glancing sideways
towards horse paddock and its vestigial
mushrooms, horses just light enough
to make something of gymkhana.
The twists and turn ignite.

As back through corners are past trees
in light burnished on spectrum's edge,
a pink-orange doused in greylight,
varieties of rust, tensions making stories
as shouts and demands to be let out
strand you always on a gravel corner,
at the thin end of a mega-burnout,
blacker than asphalt, zigzagging
over crests and sharp bends, a ledge,
devout dedication to annihilation—
the air thinner and evasive
where paddocks open out,
unreadable near mallee outcrops,
spiders pulling traps shut;
reflectors start to burn—chips
of speech, bytes of locution. By now
quarry owners would have undermined
the scarp, deceptively divided
road and habitat—admiring the view
no matter what it's built upon, admittedly
enjoying driving conditions where the road
expands. The car—a house, comfortable
in the loungeroom, legs stretched out,
steering the television—remote control
sparking its redeye like a startled
but confident animal. But there's
no comparison, and the dead litter
roads everywhere there's scrub or trees or open space
where there's pollution not yet critical,
or critical and caught in a delayed reaction.
Who are we telling this? Who changes
radials when they've run down to snarling

hooks of metal? What details
can be added from here? The close-up
lost to panorama even where trees
attempt to close over, to cut out moonlight
or sick haloes of UFOs. We've seen them,
up close—headlines that wouldn't rate
a line, like the thylacine seen at the eye
of the road, where the river is blood
in an optic nerve. I break, I swerve, I accelerate
into the curve. They seem not to want
to appreciate low ground, saltbush
and samphire, needles and Christmas spiders
that translate as tethered cities, aerial
cultures that don't come down until death:
insects caught on the mesh of the grille,
enfolded in the radiator: antifreeze and coolant,
maintaining 93 degrees centigrade as liquid
runs through the engine block, cylinder head,
the pump working as hard as a heart.
The pump as a heart? Vice versa?
Thermostat regulating flow?
Radiator: heat exchange, fins and tubes,
inlet and outlet, air flow, turbulator,
gnats, mosquitoes, flies, and dozens, possibly
hundreds of species genetically compacted,
turbulated, distance on the clock increasing,
distance home decreasing
proportionally. Petition. Ask for
information. AKA. Lexical Englishes
here to deny trails and totems,
gathering on scrubby crests, around York gums,
crossing now-time journeys and non-time

transversals: 'Wandering' is a town further south
searching for displaced letters
and categories, a metathesis, a recall
of something read, elsewhere, or cogitated,
vacantly staring at particles run together,
like painstakingly compiled sequences
for a space-flick that takes a few seconds
of screen time . . . days or weeks in the making.
Caught up on the side of the road: engine problems,
something entangled in the chassis,
a quick piss, searching back into darkness . . .
reflectors inverting impact with a roo.
The motivation and cessation of bodily functions:
there's a high road-toll on this stretch . . .
it's the weekender distances,
eye-soothing scenery, distance
between hotels and bottle shops.
Colloquial. Familiar. Dismissive—
it's dealt with like that, if not entirely forgotten,
prompted by small white crosses, a motorcycle helmet,
variable wreaths of non-cellulose flowers.
And a roo dragged into parrot bush: shreds of clothing
where the spiked leaves have hooked
a concerned passer-by. At high speed with the windows
    down
you can smell the bloating carcass. This is meat.
Occasion, survival, terror, trauma.
Seemed the dignified thing to do, what else . . . Insurance
covered it, thank God. Shoved the grille
into the radiator, crushed fins,
impaired tubes . . . those long-distance
dependencies, constrained by local

superstition, unbound by hopes of personal success—
of a faster car, of geographical distractions . . .
a holiday in the mountains, or on an island so small
there are no straight lines, only corners.

Part II

Properties that won't sell
become havens for kangaroos—large roos,
real boomers rarely seen these days—
that with enough moonlight will leap
in the headlights, have you swerve
in the manner of a decade ago,
trucks accelerating to test out
their roo bars, look for a sympathiser
in the citizen band radio, working
the confederate squelch out of static
as on the Great Eastern Highway
with miles of undulating paddocks
and struggling patches of bush
another truckie picks up, the air
relatively clear and traffic low
so late at night, or rather
in the early hours of the morning,
picks up and replies: 'you're
a real jerk . . .', but the static
pops words so it sounds like praise
and the admonished roo-killer
sails his rig over moon-coated
asphalt full of pride, of status
among his peers, his delusions

driving the lust for another roo,
another boomer, to bring down as gore,
to join the John Waters-like burlesque
of flesh and skin flapping from the roo bar,
radiator grille, not knowing that his truck
is about to be recalled because of faulty
hydraulics—the whole year's output
of that model falling prey to a weakness
in a specific part at best, in design
more likely. The smell of the paddocks
cannot be filtered by air-conditioning:
UREA, forty-six percent nitrogen . . .
high-beam violence on a corner
THAT corner, the arc that jags
and cuts into itself near Wambyn . . .
the rise, sudden descent embellishing
enhancing   excrescent   topped-up
bloated   brimming   supplemented
forced against the grain of gravel,
the insensitive or malicious who stab you
straight in the eyes, twist barbs
of gaze back into the black light trap
of sight, the two-way mirrors,
brain-scanned moon sliced
to a picture, as blind   blinded   blinding
you mnemonically follow the road,
headmap that might have been dormant
for months, even longer. Those accidents
at night without explanation—death's dazzlers,
road-edge spliced by divides, projected mallee
trees thick and heavy and making you swerve
into a fence-post, over a ledge. Or

the wild overtakers—rapid passers-by—
who cut in like a paper slice
and leave the family-wagon sailing
sailing   sailing   terror cognizant,
sailing into concrete retainer wall,
granite shoulder, hillside, tailgaters
caught in the slipstream. Delusion. Phantasm.
No metaphors to be made though it's
all connected as death is *all*'s metonym.
That lover's leap we pass quickly—
where perching allows Mediterranean delusions
on the scarp, the place where the murderer
of blacks had the tables—his tables
of stats, land accrual, harvests, sheep guts,
hogget, lambs, hay stooks   maybe
maybe turned as tables in a dining room
that bitterly resented campfires, dances,
songs with words that had neither
beginning or end, that reached
through white skin sideways,
as if it wasn't there, straight to the heart
which felt it all but didn't know
what to do with it but kick back
angrily, like rifle shots, jaws or roo dogs.
Premeditation was built into the culture
of 'settlement'. He was chased
and leapt to his death to escape,
which he did, connected to the song
without beginning, without end.
Shit! I didn't dip my lights,
I hope it didn't dazzle them too much . . .
I know what it's like. Do you think

I should go back to check? Having rounded
the bend I can't see anything in my mirrors.
No, you're probably right, I've got
to work on this paranoia, not let
it get the better of me. Actually,
I was distracted by the irony
of Malcolm Lowry's poem 'Happiness'.
'Trees with branches rooted in air . . .'
In daylight you can clearly see where the runoff
has washed the soil away from roots
of York gums and mallees—the roots
make confused and awkward extensions
to the trunks, or simply lash out
at crisp deposits of salt when it's dry.
That's *now*, we're passing the exact spot:
old hippy commune with heaps
of shattered asbestos, fibres
catching in sheoak brushes,
a generator on the brink of seizure.
So I was thinking ahead of myself
when that car sailed head-on
into my high beam, one map
overlaid another and I made an error
of judgement. A mistake. Or maybe
my consciousness being so removed
from the here and now—the there and then—
that another set of laws were governing
my mood, a magic realism
not measurable by the sort
of blood-tests or blow-bags
they have in their arsenal. Unsighted,
not even lit up by the sharpest

of spotlights. We pass the shed
where that guy stuck his dick
through the abrasive disk of a grinding paper,
calling it a frilled-necked lizard—but that
might have happened somewhere else,
an old trick. A utility varies its speed
by twenty or thirty, still twenty
or thirty below the speed limit
when peaking—overtaking
you find it accelerates to the speed limit
and beyond, blocking your return,
double white lines and a bend
leaving you nowhere to go,
a head-on brewing as headlights
lack definition. Just escaping.
The utility drops back to its old patterns
and pins in the mirror, shedding
anthropomorphics . . . Quarry trucks
keep on dragging on, carting
marginal land and a rhetoric
that displaces imagery of accidents.

CONFESSION

If flesh extends to open air, clearings
in woodland, do I ingest the auras
                                    of the flitting
silhouettes released from resin, from amber?
Heavy clouds are linked to my eyes,

and plume like squid-ink
in the seas off Busselton.
                    The skin on my palms
wets as gravel, leaving taint or impression: wheat sheaves
against this backdrop as escutcheon,
                            as if I mocked honour,
or failed to walk the winding ways of turrets
in what they say, as vertigo: embraced, and old-world.
This order of angels,
                    bones they toss in gambles,
sentient rebuff,
                    quoting sacred cows, rapid enough
to fuse the nerves, a ministry of horror.
                            I shut myself off
across the terrazzo woodland floor, the houses
it will make. Sweetened tanks of dozers,
                        mine own
stenographer: see these keepsakes named as pews,
cushions to soften prayers. Doesn't it make sense
for a pacifist to listen to aggressive music?
                        To praise
the hoax and all kinds of levity.
                    The male and female
elegant parrot look barely different, or not as different
as the male and female red-capped parrot . . .
                        the horn-shaped
buds of the wandoo are branding-irons to me, scalding
and marking, incriminating as farmland
or quarries; my queries are tossed from one text
to the next and there's too much rewriting,
reconfiguring of lost species,
                        transitional tendencies.

SALT IS PART OF THE ENVIRONMENT

Slightly lower than the coast
though two hours' drive or a few days'
walk at an angle to the rising sun,
the sunset cutting in like fear
or a reminder of loss, a codicil,
swamp-patches eat into scrubland
at rare points where clearing
has failed, or been avoided.
These places are often saline.
It's what demographers
might call natural salt depression,
the water table divulging itself
within the fabric of plant growth,
like bio-necessity. Clearing melaleucas
and flooded gums, the big drinkers,
it extends—naturally—up from recession
into planar surfaces: paddocks,
house yards, catching pens.
This is what we'd expect,
and there's no alchemy
or surprise attacks in this.
Between York and Tammin
you can see that a house and sheds
not far from the bitumen
have been eaten almost entirely
by salt-frosting reaching up out

of the wet; it aches most in the heat
when the sparkle of salt is a mirage
of moisture, calenture the only
return on thirst. The equation
doesn't balance—quirky
like the animals who inhabit
these places. Condemned to trial
by media, written up
by the 'all that glisters is not gold'
school of journalism.

SALT SEMI-ODE

Maligned but part of the place,
the city feeds on rural disgrace,
tendrils of learning reach out
into the wheatbelt, and devout

critics research remnant bushland
until seeds can no longer purchase sand,
and science becomes art as poets
build Sodom and Gomorrah, and visionary boats

sail out on halcyon mirages,
all colours played by crystals,
shimmering blankness and wire-rust gauges,
poverty and sadness as expansion stalls.

SALT IS THE RESIDUE OF HAUNTINGS

Spiritualist episodes, the matter
collecting on the colonial parlour's floor,
occasion for neighbours and visiting dignitaries,
son or daughter of a marriageable family, visiting,
match up like orange light enraptured in salt-ice
after the vicious heat of mid-summer,
these early traces of the cause célèbre
of the early twenty-first century.
It's even got into the graves,
our inverted bogeyman, ghosting the surface
like their indomitable spirits tree-cutting,
ploughing, winning at cricket, developing
something quicker than rugby,
more assertive than Gaelic football; no corpse
stuck in the ground, or floating on springs
of clear water. Blood is the rust of crops
harbouring grudges against the season
on the cusp of Christmas, furious
with storms and cutthroat prices,
rigorous grain-sampling standards,
the central economy of co-operative
bulk handling . . . a wealth of ectoplasm
exchanged for the bag count of lost years.

DUSK AND THE BODY POLITIC

Machinery works furrows of sound
as the light is barely enough to sustain,
furtive flowers lately opening,
brief in the spectrum leap
between yellow and blue,
a colour that sounds as both
merged true, its collusion science
or elicitation, the motor's torque
as the crankshaft drives heavy rubber,
split differentials of earthmoving,
the smallest of birds still calling,
to be heard over the noise
that fibrillates with distance and fluids
of darkness, the nightjar undercutting
chirrups, ominous range-finder
and operatic singer of low and medium gears,
cogs of flesh and bone turned as planets.

HIVES

Hive off gold-bronze light
that isn't a colour but a spray-on
adhesive with a short half-life,
Wallaby Hills a place in a ritualised

conversation, so he feels satisfied
that he's getting his money's worth
given that his offer of a trade-off
(no deposit) foundered like a paddock
against wattle and salmon gums,
dryandra and tight-twists of mallee;
in the abutting farm, among
cities of termites, the scrupulous rows
of white beehives, bringing to mind
the fluted prison of Judith Wright,
or some earlier poem you wrote
in teenage years, influenced
by Wright's poem; hives funnelling
and the odd bee at sunset elusive
as freedom, to fly back to manipulation,
golden deaths tainted with black
and unprocessed pollen, the silent spikes,
the stings that'll heal and kill,
antihistamines building up in the system,
sandy soil rehabilitation in this place
where orchids might come again
this year, adding taste
to a prisoner's diet.

LIKE SLIVERS OF GLASS . . .

Like slivers of glass
the hairs on the stem
of Paterson's Curse
lodge in the skin

sitting unnoticed
until rubbed contrary,
a reversed lint brush
with bite, perverse

as seasonal: wintergrowth
making the stemhairs softer,
the pulling hand wrapped 'round
to purify the garden

as more sexual seasons
approach and sting you, almost
transparent and part of you
loving, walking . . .

it being easier to long for . . .
when elsewhere, a skin irritation
that thrives on discomfort,
convinces with its efficacy

though a rash of conscience
emerges like an eruption of skin cells,
a hair implantation
where the garden is bare

waiting for freshly sown seed
to rise in replacement,
follow the sun,
grow with the grain.

UNDER THE VOLCANO

'We discard the horripilation of the weather . . .'
—MALCOLM LOWRY

Three white-faced herons arrive this morning,
the extinct volcano weathered down to the emollient
of mist and oil of eucalypt, spiralling
on to the limbs of their roosting tree, body fed
on soakage and samphire, their deep-throated croak
the result of scandal or espionage, swaying
as the dregs of the front stir the mist and gently
whip the leaves, but never at risk
of unseating. This overloading of presence,
as if to collude spirits bring a triple
assignation or confirmation or warning,
the sodden ground humus or hubris or bog people
not as constrained as in the place surveyors
came from. The ungainly leave-taking is rhythmic,
and we can't deny the mood falters regardless.

SITE

for Jonathan Bate

We look for that point of contact
that crops up in conversation or letters
or in surveys of vocation;
                    slow blood
pushing its way round, as if the tunnels before
its limp walls are hollow, expectant.
                              The purple-veined
spider orchid is a nerve centre, powerboard
we'll plug into from wherever; steel-capped boots
trample underfoot: wood collectors, shooters,
kids tracking enemies. Where enemies
come from varies with technology;
                         who writes,
who apportions part of their attention span,
cries just because the music is in a minor key.
                                   Have you seen
the red leschenaultia flowering in islands, focal
cascades amongst the kwongan?
                        The pupils fire
and the site pales as further away.
                         Perfidy, ripple
of muscles and component parts urging
a gushing out, a bleeding heart. This is every
one of you built up to a head, to my lungs

so tight I barely breathe, my hands and feet
all maps overlaid, cratered, furrowed, riven, creased;
shadow linked to shadow linked to shadow,
                                        an anthology
of creed and intentionality. Signals, cages, beacons,
the chrysalis of an unopened pink sunray,
or fields in which poisons weren't understood,
but that's childhood.
                        Forty years doles out inlays
and extractions, the draining rock
above cave systems that even now harbour
species of animals unknown to anybody—anybody
at all. Out here, sight shuts down;
inside, scant light amplifies.

GLOW

for Tracy

Filling the space
of the birds that were
but have left, or gone into hiding,
unless so localised a habitat
precludes evidence,
or implicates a need
in us, not me, I rarefy
objects spread out on my
evening walk home,
that roosting time

would be semi-silent,
trapped in dusk-lull,
forced to be metrical
as my blood reaches out,
warms the parameters
of our encirclement.

DEATH OF A BRUSHTAIL POSSUM

In the valley, on granite faces,
cosseted by sheoak perimeters,
lichen, moss, black run-off,
a brushtail possum broken down,
strewn over and into cracks—
a limb, vertebrae, envelope of skin and fur,
touched by a boot, an undoing
touching both, that makes the granite
as overcast as clouds already
infested by gravity, the pull-down
levity a host to temperature—
cold, yet sultry, the ghost-imaging
it engenders . . . more blood
in the emptied body than on
the distant road, ripping with traffic.
Yellow robins and dusky wood swallows
cite a ministry of antithesis over this island
of all that's been said, plus acacias, flowering dryandra,
the white-fleshed granite that uncaps
a grey expression, the blank ink

they sign in deflection,
all here with the remains
of the possum—fox victim.

SURFACE HISTORIES: A TOWN IN THE WHEATBELT

1.

The horse rails gone, then back again,
an auntie tries the wheel
of a car that looks almost the same—

searching for gears
in an automatic, and caught
by the realisation

that gesturing remains
incapable of prompting
the internal combustion engine

to connect, to drive
the analogue, to drive the main street
of town, and realising her mistake

an error of visual
and spatial judgement, as if they
could ever be separated

detected her own car
two parking spaces away:
same colour, same model

but manual version
in the town where all cars
are known by family name.

2.

It begins and ends
in some ways
with the closing of the banks.

With weekend dalliances
with historic cars, and shady pasts.
Boutique hotels

are softened out of hard drinking,
exteriors of bad seasons
washed away.

Mains power, scheme water,
the old court house
a museum.

It's all settlers
and cottage industries
only an hour's drive

from the city.

3.

Recalling childhood
doesn't mean nostalgia,
even if swinging out on a rope

into the Avon brings pleasure.
Amoebic meningitis, those caught
by snags and roots.

4.

They move into town when kids
take over the properties,
or when they've sold up.

Living under the shadow of Mount Bakewell,
in the vicinity of their former activities.
High roofs keep old houses cool

on the slopes of Mount Brown,
and the trucks roll past
on their way to the bins.

That old man buying groceries
is Uncle Jack, his wife dead,
the farm broken up,

he's hard of hearing and frail.
He's a diviner, though I don't know
if the electricity's still with him.

5.

They're developing land out back
on the edge of the river: for years
claims were made to the Shire

and turned down. But parcels
are being doled out now
and someone's making a packet:

Councils come and go.

6.

The farmer's co-op
stocks tractor parts and bullets.
The company that owns it

has underwritten
the purchase and curation
of a great art collection:

of Australian art,
of home, hearth, and nation
of course.

7.

'There's less racism here
because we don't want to talk about it.'
Not sure where to go with this . . .

It seems history steps in
and locals' 'stories' are 'celebrated'.
There are a variety of histories,

and the lines of the Wagyl are clearly there
for those who know or want to know
where to look.

A variety of nationalities
attend the Catholic church, you'll hear,
though 'not in great numbers'.

Location set up
to speak for itself . . .

8.

Balladong Farm
is not owned by hippies,
despite bare feet and an avoidance

of pesticides. 'New money
is temporary', it is said in town,
'they've let it go to seed'.

The riverbank under their protection
is growing back again, foxes and rabbits
dialogue and the native birds flourish.

Heritage buildings work as studios,
and small dramas are played out
in the theatre.

9.

On the edge of town
the birds come: at the town's heart
they cull with guns.

The birdcall is saturation:
you can see it, the white corellas
change colour as they intone:

the red of their blood
hazing paddocks,
bringing blood vessels

to the surface.
Consanguinity.
Rose-coloured glasses.

10.

Holy Trinity,
locus for an aspect of community.
There are other churches,

other nationalities within nation.
I guess all said prayers
when the young girl

was lost on the railway line.
Her beliefs are best known by her family.
Wreaths still hang on the crossing: fresh, vital.

11.

That lot's got tickets on themselves,
they're up themselves,
and they're as rough as guts.

Think they're special,
he drinks and she shoplifts,
haven't heard of contraception,

so much money they don't know what to do with it,
rich cockies, dole scroungers,
a decent family of hard workers—

their daughter worked in the shop
before going to the city
to study, mix with the wrong crowd.

12.

That brother hasn't talked to the other
in thirty years, despite only the railway
and a vacant block dividing their houses.

They'd already stopped when settling
on their building spots: keeping an eye

out through the silence, seeing
what the other's got. One day
someone will build the vacant plot

out, though it's likely
a paper trail will lead to one or both of them,
the weeds and odd York gum

safe until they've given up the ghost,
lost sight of each other
through the growth.

13.

The windows
of real-estate offices
offer

that weekend retreat:
good water,
a view,

only a touch of salt.
Tourists come in buses
and cars, the latter

watched closely
by realtors. The bush block—increasingly rare,
the hobby farm—a fad from the 70s,

the horse plot—an active local racing industry
studded with 'identities',
the stone house not far

from the river—cellars cool
to stock their wines. Turnover
is high. Weekend retreats

are commodities
that change hands rapidly.
Quid faciat laetas segetes. . . .

14.

Festival. Carnivale.
The sheep in the fields
embodied.

Harpsichords in the earliest houses,
jazz in the town hall,
the end of year dance.

A reporter from the *Chronicle*
collects names of those he doesn't recognise—
they come from a far way out,

and there's a percentage
of the population that floats,
shifts. A vegan won a baking prize

for a chocolate applesauce cake
in the great halls of bounty
last year. The keepers

tasted without knowing
the absence of eggs and dairy.
The silent revolution.

15.

Money saved
in closing down
the youth centre

is spent on repairs
and the publicity
descrying an increase

in vandalism.
The gods of Rome
were lost with its statues.

16.

Drinkers see a different town.
As if they've got special insight
and can clearly see the dead

and lost occupying
the same space
as the living.

17.

There are still panel vans
in Australia, and they gather
in the gravel carpark

opposite the Castle pub
on Friday and Saturday nights.
They risk burnouts,

and blokes have it off
with chicks in the back.
The blokes say 'she's a good root',

or call her a bush pig if they don't get it.
There are sluts in town,
but their side of the story is elsewhere.

18.

Old families: 'settler' and Nyungar,
are spoken of with reverence or hatred.
There seems to be no indifference,

at least behind closed doors
everyone has an opinion.
Nyungars remember the names

of the whites who didn't murder
as much as those who did. White
families are mostly proud

of 'treating them right'
and take pride in the production
of footballers. Nyungar people

take pride as well,

but for different reasons,
also, and at least.

19.

Anonymity of GM trials.
Landcare for increased profitability.
Red Bull girls

turning it on for the bike trials.
The roo in Doc Jones' yard
and the heronry

near the old railway bridge.
The destruction of the only
alpine bushland

in the wheatbelt.
A pair of black-shouldered kites
nesting just beyond

the point beyond
which they'll deliver
no mail.

Voting in the school classrooms.
Field days and chaff in the air.
Gradations of heat.

'HUNG LIKE A HORSE'

You know they say
she's not as sweet
as the honeysuckles
she coaxes over the walls
of her house, as delicate
as the everlastings
she lets run rampant
in paddocks
left fallow year
after year; they say
the man who shacked
up with her those months
was hung like a horse:
that he went in to put
things right: plough
paddocks, clean out
the shed, strain
fences. He'd tell
his mates that he rode
her into the ground
and that she bucked
like crazy. 'I put
a smile on her face'.
Cast out, he never
looks up from his drink.
He can't convince

the guys at the piss tray
that he loved her
entirely.

THE WEDDING ECLOGUE

Groom

The luck in seeing you addressed
by wagtail and twenty-eight parrot, my seedy
Best Man who's half-cut before
the first run of the morning,
lacklustre skies semi-brewing
a storm that'd finish off crops
in a tight season, but is full
of mockery instead. When the Armada
was scattered by the winds
the English believed it was God himself
blew their Catholic arses off-line:
I apologise to the other side
of your family, angry because
we're in the wrong church,
but as your mother is paying
I guess they can take a running
jump. The way those parrot shrieks
hook into each other like barbed wire,
or interlock mesh, or twists of an auger.

Bride

It's a concession, I never
wanted a church wedding, wearing
this off-blue after years of fucking.
We were married in all but law
ten years ago. Maybe now Social
Security and bar-sluts and macho-bastards
at the pool table will show respect.
I sound like you! The lace in this dress
just isn't me. Know what you mean—
always know what you mean—
about the shrieks of those birds.
Cut into you, but in a sickly
sweet kind of way. A choir,
that only cuts a bit.

Groom

I'll finish the shed tomorrow
and then we'll hightail it south,
to a steady cool place where tall trees
monitor sunlight and birdcall
is softened around the edges.
The coast is ragged and furious,
and the weight of the world
is driven back, but it's out of focus,
and there's something vague,
like your skin—you know
what I mean . . . soft-ish,
almost sexual.

Bride

This sprig of everlastings
will ward off bad luck—we should
have kept away from each other
just before the ceremony.
In some cultures the whole town
waits outside until blood's drawn . . .

Groom

That'd suit this town of perverts!
Bit late for us, but we'll put on
some kind of show. Harvest
isn't far off—at least the spray
clouds have come and gone.

Bride

Listen to that flock of pink and greys
coming in over the hills. On time.
They fly in complex arrangements:
their rhythms don't complement
the wedding procession—and for that
we should be glad. Driving south,
we'll pass the storm-tongued
black cockatoos. A warning,
knee-jerk reaction. They can't
stand us in this town. But

then again, not expecting to hear
strains of the golden whistler,
will bring them singing
over your doorstep,
calling to help put out a fire
on a neighbouring farm.

ENVOY

AMONG THE MURK I WILL FIND
THINGS TO WORSHIP

Among the murk I will find things to worship,
the memory dressed up in acrylics, dawn-
haze training scrub on the mountain, bird-exchange
    tossed up around them.

That probity will move independently
rocks the river redgum, roots set down below
the salt line, a monoplane grinding the air,
    droning tepid clouds.

Christ, down-wind, picks up the static, facing us—
offers least resistance; down in the city
we eat with the Buddhists, admire the Jewish
    critic in traffic.

Amid sheoaks the Prophet stirs the thornbill,
the galahs cut their jagged about-face flight,
rust and oily residue slick the river,
    and yet, deny them!

The old man has lost his farm, moved into town—
huddles in the kitchen, Metters Stove burning
low, rubs the emblem from his tractor's bonnet,
    calling heaven down.